50 TIPS TO BECOME A SUCCESSFUL ENTREPRENEUR

The Ultimate
BUSINESS
OWNER'S
MANUAL

TERRY MONROE

AN INC.
ORIGINAL

An Inc. Original
New York, New York
www.anincoriginal.com

Copyright © 2024 Terry Monroe

This work is being published under the An Inc. Original imprint by an exclusive arrangement with Inc. Magazine. Inc. Magazine and the Inc. logo are registered trademarks of Mansueto Ventures, LLC. The An Inc. Original logo is a wholly owned trademark of Mansueto Ventures, LLC.

Distributed by River Grove Books

Design and composition by Greenleaf Book Group
Cover design by Greenleaf Book Group

Publisher's Cataloging-in-Publication data is available.

Print ISBN: 978-1-63909-041-9

eBook ISBN: 978-1-63909-042-6

First Edition

Contents

CONTENTS

PREFACE

Ever since I can remember, I have always wanted to be in business. I wasn't sure what kind of business I wanted to be in and definitely didn't know how I was going to be in business, since nobody in my family had ever been in business for themselves. We were a working-class family from the southernmost part of Illinois, and the best anyone in our family could hope for was to get a good job. If you graduated from high school, this was considered higher education.

I got my first taste of business when I was in the fifth grade, and I became a newspaper boy. I would ride my bike to the newspaper office as soon as school was out, pick up my newspapers from the printing press, then fold the newspapers, put them in my delivery bag that went on the handlebars of my bicycle, and ride from house to house throwing newspapers onto my customers' porches. I did this every day regardless of whether it was raining or snowing—because you had to deliver your product to your customers. Because I was responsible for money that was owed to the newspaper office for the newspapers I had picked up on consignment and had to pay my bill back, I would go to each of my customers' homes every Saturday and knock on the door to collect the money my customers owed me for the papers I delivered throughout the previous week. If my bill with the newspaper office was $30.00 and I only collected $25.00, the difference came out of my pocket. Therefore, at the ripe old age of 11, I learned not only how to sell but also how to collect money and balance my account. I also remember knocking on people's doors, them hiding inside their house to avoid paying me, and having to go several weeks before I would get my money. Maybe this is why I never liked having businesses with accounts receivables.

Even though I had no idea I was in business when I was a newspaper boy, I loved delivering newspapers and the idea of being in business, meeting new people, interacting with customers, and making money.

When I was in the seventh grade, my family moved to another town where I finished high school. My family was not a proponent of going to college, because they had not gone to college, but instead promoted the idea of getting a good job. Well, after having over a dozen jobs during high school, I found myself at 19 years old with a good job in the best factory in town and married to my high school sweetheart. I thought I had arrived and that there was nothing else to do but have a family and keep working at the factory, which I did for 10 years, and I hated it. I would daydream about being in business for myself. I told myself I could be a businessperson. I had no formal training to be in business and had no clue where to start, but I knew I wanted to be in business for myself.

After 10 years of working in the factory (by the way, I worked in three factories before I learned I didn't like working in a factory), I got my lucky break and was able to quit my job and go into business with my dad, who was in the oil business. I was in charge of the sales department and finance part of the business. (There were only three people in the company, to give you an idea of how big our oil company was.) I was underqualified and had no idea how to operate a business, but it didn't matter—I was out of the factory, and I was in business and didn't have to punch a time clock.

The oil business was good to me for about four years until the price of oil crashed and we started losing money, but I wasn't too worried, because by then I was already in another business, and it was growing like crazy, and I was making enough money that I didn't have to go back to the factory to work.

Fast forward, and over the course of time, I became a self-taught serial entrepreneur owning over 40 different businesses. It didn't make any difference as to what kind of business it was, I just loved owning and operating businesses. I used to say I had a disease for a long time called "dealitis," meaning I couldn't pass up a deal. I would buy or start a business I thought was a good idea at the time. Overall, I have owned service businesses such as real estate brokerage companies, a television station, a radio station, convenience stores, liquor stores, a ladies clothing store, a construction company, a motel, 32 restaurants of different types and brands, retail electronic stores, video rental stores, and hundreds of oil wells. I started my own franchise company, and I have owned 10 different assorted national franchises. I grew one business from one retail store to 155 stores in 27 states and Canada before taking it public. Eventually I sold all of the businesses to get into becoming an intermediary specializing in helping family-owned businesses prepare their businesses for sale and market them to the public.

My love for being in business and working with business owners has never waned, and because of my love for business, I was able to write the book you are about to read.

If you are presently in business or thinking about getting

into business, then you should read this book. All the content from this book came from personal experiences of what to do and what not to do. It covers the good, the bad, and sometimes the ugliness of business. I write this book to help people not get blindsided by many of the issues that will come upon or happen to them while on their business journey. Some of the things I write about you may already know, and therefore this book is a good reminder. But I can assure you there are some things that you do not know and would never think could happen, and that is what I want you to be prepared for. I hope you enjoy reading my business tips and continue to enjoy being in business.

INTRODUCTION

What you are about to read is a compilation of my 40+ years of experience with starting businesses, buying businesses, selling businesses, and managing over a thousand employees. In the pages ahead, you will get my top 50 tips on succeeding in business. At times, my advice on managing employees or businesses may come across as harsh or cynical. And that would be a pretty fair assumption. (You don't get to where I am in business without becoming a little—or in my case a lot—cynical.)

It is not in my nature to sugarcoat things. I am direct and call it how I see it. I also believe that when I pick up a book like this, I should be able to find at least one or two nuggets of wisdom that will help me in my business by saving me some time, money, or grief, ultimately leaving me in a better position than when I started the book. To help you find a few of your own nuggets of wisdom, I've created action items at the end of each chapter to reinforce what you are reading.

If you are presently in business, I commend you, because if someone has never experienced owning and operating their own business, they have no idea how lonely, yet gratifying, it can be. When you are in business, you are alone. The success of a business will ultimately depend on you. Sure, there may be a spouse, a partner, or a key employee who works with you in the business, but in reality, it is you alone who will determine if the business is a success.

Anyone who has been successful or has failed in business will look inside themselves for what went right or what went wrong with the business. Unfortunately, when things go right a lot of businesspeople think the success of the business was solely because of their talents, when in retrospect a large part of the business's success was due to being in the right place at the right time and not having any substantial competition. Since we can't always bank on luck, I wrote this book to help you, whether you are just beginning your venture or you are a more seasoned entrepreneur. So, if you're ready to get started, let's turn the page and look at the first tip.

PART 1

—

Starting Out

Tip #1

CREATE A BUSINESS PLAN

A business plan can be simple. It doesn't have to be something like a college MBA would create. You can get sample business plans on the internet for free. But what a simple business plan does is give you a written guide as to what kind of business you are in, where you want to go, and how you plan to get there. Basically, it is a map to help guide you where you want to go with your business. It is no different than if you were going on a trip and needed a map—or in today's world, a GPS—to show you how to get somewhere.

I used to think writing a business plan was only for people who were going to be building a sophisticated business and therefore I didn't need one—when in reality I was just being lazy. The first business plan I wrote was terrible. In fact, it was embarrassing. I was trying to become a vendor to Walmart. Yes, Walmart, the largest retailer in the world. I had made it through the maze of people to the individual I needed to talk to in order to become a vendor, and the person in charge said they would consider allowing me and my company to be a vendor to Walmart, but I needed to send him a business plan.

"

Writing down your thoughts into a business plan solidifies your intention and retention.

I had no idea how to create a business plan, so I purchased a computer program for business plans and filled in the blanks with why I should be a vendor to Walmart. The plan I wrote could have been written by an eighth grader (it was that bad), but I had a plan, and it worked, and I got the opportunity to become a vendor to Walmart, which turned into a very successful endeavor. Since then, I learned to always have a business plan. It may only be a few pages long, but it is your own thoughts and ideas on paper, and it helps guide you in the direction you need to go.

Don't try to do this in your head and work off your thoughts. It must be in written or typed form so you can read it and refer to it. Writing down your thoughts into a business plan solidifies your intention and retention.

It is all changeable, but without a business plan you are a "wandering generality" instead of a "meaningful specific," and you will not stay the course.

TAKING ACTION

Keep things simple. When writing your business plan, start and begin with a list of bullet points you want to accomplish with your business. For example, if you want to create a business that is about pets or gardening, determine your audience, how you will market, and how you will grow your customer base:

- My target audience will be baby boomers aged 55 and older.
- My main form of marketing will be internet advertising.
- New content will be added weekly and shared with my customers.
- I will invite customers' input to help broaden my customer base.
- I will join the association applicable to my business.

Continue creating your list of ideas and then compile your list into a business plan.

Tip #2

FOCUS ON SALES

Always, always, always focus on sales. If you remember nothing else, remember this: Without sales there is no business. When I say sales, I am also referring to the top line of your profit and loss (P&L) statements, which relate to income. From the time you wake up until the time you close your eyes at night, your waking thoughts should always be about sales and how to make the top line bigger. I say this because if the income of the business is not large enough, then you have no business. You can cut costs only so far and then you are out of business.

———————————— " ————————————

**From the time you wake up until
the time you close your eyes at night,
your waking thoughts should always
be about sales and how to make
the top line bigger.**

———————————————

You must have certain costs to keep the doors open. We call these the hard costs needed to operate, or you may have heard someone say, "cracking the nut," meaning once the business has generated enough income to cover the hard costs and keep the business operating, generally a large portion of any additional income will flow to the bottom line and be considered profits. And with sales there is no limit. It doesn't matter if you are in the service business or the manufacturing business. High sales can generally fix any type of problem in business. Low sales are the number-one reason businesses fail. Every day you operate, your business sales should be your number-one priority.

TAKING ACTION

It's time to put your current sales strategy to the test.

- Jot down your current sales goals. Be realistic as to where you are today and where you will be in 6 months, 12 months, 1 year, and 3 years. Be sure to make a list of HOW you are going to meet these goals; otherwise, you are just making a wish list that may or may not be realized.

  » Are you meeting or exceeding these goals? If not, what steps can you take to remedy this?

- Now, take a hard look at your current sales strategy.

  » What is one thing you can do today to increase your sales this month?

  » Pretend you are the customer and think about what items or services you will need. Then implement those ideas.

- Revisit your goals in a month to see if they are being met.

Tip #3

KEEP GOOD BOOKS
AND RECORDS

It goes without saying that when you are in business, you must know if you are making money or not. The best way to find this out is by keeping good books and records. Good books and records will track all your income and expenses. This goes beyond just looking into your checkbook or bank account to see if you have money in there. Having (or not having) good books and records will determine if you are able to get a bank loan, attract investors, and more importantly, stay in business. Also, if you ever decide to sell the business, you will need good books and records to get its full value.

———————— " ————————

Having (or not having) good books and records will determine if you are able to get a bank loan, attract investors, and more importantly, stay in business.

All too often people will start a business out of their house or garage, and the business will grow into one that is highly profitable. What happens is as the business grows, it also changes, and the way you keep track of your income and expenses will also change.

In the beginning you may have been able to operate the business out of your checkbook, and since it was just you, there was no need to have an accounting system or an accountant because you were only reporting to yourself, and you knew exactly how much money you were making. But as your business grows, so do the systems that are needed to help track its growth.

I have seen individuals who had grown their business in excess of $10,000,000 a year in sales underestimate the need for good books and records only to realize they could not grow the business any further due to the inadequacy of their poor accounting system. Their negligence in not implementing good accounting books and records ultimately forced them to sell their business for a lesser amount than it was worth.

When I mention to someone that they will need good books and records to maintain and grow a profitable business, their first response is that they have an accountant, and everything will be alright. But just because they have an accountant does not negate the fact that all an accountant can do is put the system in place and input the information they are provided. Therefore, if you are not providing the correct information to the accountant, all you will have are some P&L statements that are incorrect, which makes things even worse.

I once owned a multimillion-dollar business spanning multiple states in the United States. My books were so bad that my CPA and his accounting firm quit working for me because of the bad information I had been providing them. Yes, I had books and records, but they were worthless because they were all incorrect due to my ignorance of the need for good financial systems and the role they play in the daily performance of a business. The outcome of this situation was I ultimately had to pay over $400,000 to the Arthur Andersen accounting firm to get my books and records in order before I could even sell the business. And to make matters worse,

I had to take a discount on the sale of the business due to having poor books and records.

The moral of this story is you cannot rely on your accountant to take care of everything when ultimately you are responsible for the information that you give them. The buck always does stop with you if it is your business. So do yourself and your business a favor, and make sure your books (and records) are in order.

TAKING ACTION

Take a look at your books and records and ask yourself:

- Are they up to date?
- Are they in order?
- Would *you* buy your business after reviewing your books and records?
    - » If not, what steps can you take today to remedy this?
- Check back next quarter to assess the state of your books and records.
    - » Are things better or worse? It has to be one or the other because nothing stays the same.
    - » Then do what is needed to fix the problem to avoid bigger problems down the road.

Tip #4

DON'T SKIM

For those who have never heard the word, "skimming" is a term that is generally used when the owner of a business who handles a lot of cash transactions decides they are not going to report all the cash on their books and records and instead puts the cash into their pocket to avoid paying taxes on the income. The idea of skimming has been around since taxation was invented.

However, what a lot of business owners do not know is the taxing authorities have a set of guidelines that tell them how much a business should be paying for the cost of goods and how much the business should be bringing to the bottom line as a net profit. If a business owner is "skimming" money from the incoming sales and reducing the overall income but still expensing the cost of goods, the percentage of cost of goods to sales will be out of whack and noticeable by the taxing authorities. This is a prime way for a lot of business owners to get themselves in trouble. Not only will skimming get you in trouble with the taxing authorities, but it will also reduce the amount of money you will be paid for the business when you decide you want to sell it.

If the cash flow from the business was never recorded in the books, you can't expect a buyer to pay you for something you cannot prove. What we say is you can't get paid for something twice. By that we mean if you don't show your income on your books and records, you're telling a buyer that you have been skimming. By making such a "statement" to a prospective buyer, you are not only letting the buyer know that you have been cheating the government by not reporting all of your business income, but you are also letting them know that you cannot be trusted because you are a thief.

———————————— " ————————————

Not only will skimming get you in trouble with the taxing authorities, but it will also reduce the amount of money you will be paid for the business when you decide you want to sell it.

Another downside to skimming is if you should ever need to go to a bank and get a loan for the business or something in your personal life, the value of the business will be reduced, and your ability to acquire a loan would be jeopardized. And I don't believe it would be wise to tell a bank loan officer that you are skimming, aka stealing from the government, while you are trying to convince them you are of good character. If you were a loan officer, would you trust this person with your bank's money to help them grow their business?

—————————— 66 ——————————

You can't get paid for something twice.

Something a lot of people don't know is that it is getting harder to spend a large amount of cash and purchase large ticket items. For example, if you're in a trade or business and receive more than $10,000 in cash in a single transaction or in related transactions, you must file Form 8300. The IRS uses Form 8300 to track large cash payments and suspicious transactions to prevent money laundering and other such crimes. This is why title companies no longer accept cash, thereby disallowing an individual to purchase real estate through a title company with cash. Many other business establishments are following suit and have decided not to accept cash in response to the government's requirement of having to file forms for cash transactions.

As you can see, skimming has multiple negative repercussions, and we're just skimming the surface here (pun intended). So, regardless of how tempting it may be to have a lot of cash in your hands, don't skim. Ever.

TAKING ACTION

As the owner of your company, you must report all income earned. If someone else is keeping your books, take active measures to ensure that your income is being reported properly by requesting detailed P&L statements. I would recommend quarterly statements at a minimum; however, monthly would be better.

This ongoing review accomplishes a few things:

- You are letting your bookkeeper (and management) know you are monitoring your business cash flow.

- This creates a culture of financial accountability that enables you to oversee how your business is being run.

- It also gives you the opportunity to notice and get clarification on questionable expenses before they become legal problems that could result in IRS penalties or, worse, jail time.

- It helps you maintain a healthy line of credit with lenders.

This assures them and prospective buyers that you are running a reputable company, which will reward you handsomely in the long term (when you sell your business) while also helping you grow your business in the short term.

Tip #5

ALWAYS PAY YOUR TAXES ON TIME

Many times, when things get tough and there may not be enough cash flow to pay all the costs of the business, people think they can let the government slide and not pay their taxes on time, whether they are sales taxes, employment taxes, withholding taxes, or local taxes. The thought behind this kind of behavior is generally that the government has more money than I do, and I need the money more than them, so they can just wait for their money. Although this statement is true, it does not mean you should practice such a thing.

Not paying your taxes when they are due falls under the category of delusion, because the money belongs to these taxing agencies and the penalty for not paying your taxes promptly not only costs you financially, but also runs the risk of having your business shut down. Did you know that taxing authorities can reach into your bank account without your consent and take the money that is owed to them? Think about it: They have your account numbers. And you didn't warn them that you were going to be late, so they feel entitled to leave you in the dark when they reach into your account and take their money. I know you don't want to hear this, but this does happen. And though it's dirty pool, the banks will not stop them.

———————— **"** ————————

Did you know that taxing authorities can reach into your bank account without your consent and take the money that is owed to them?

If you thought that was disturbing, here's another tidbit to remember. The result of the government reaching into your account without your knowledge is that any outstanding checks you may have written (should they exceed your account balance) will not be covered by your bank (unless you have overdraft protection). When you overdraw, your checks will bounce and result in penalties, not just from your bank, but from the taxing agencies as well.

But wait. There's more! This creates an even bigger problem: Now you have vendors or individuals or payroll checks that are not being paid, because you elected not to pay your taxes on time, and the government wanted their money and came and got it. If you think your employees and vendors will be sympathetic, think again!

There may be situations where you do not have the money to pay all the taxes that are owed, which is why the government does have a payment plan. But be aware if you decide to use the government as a bank and make payments, the interest and penalty costs are considerably more than a normal bank would charge. Why does the government charge you such high interest and penalties? Because they can! So, do yourself and your business a favor and pay your taxes on time.

TAKING ACTION

No one likes paying taxes, but the reality is it's something we all have to do. To avoid getting behind on your payments, create a schedule and stick to it. Some people like to jot the dates down on their calendars. Others do better adding it to their phone and email calendars. Whatever works for you, pick that. Then stick with it.

Tip #6

KNOW YOUR BUSINESS ENTITIES

I don't pretend to be an accountant, even though I have worked with accountants for over 40 years and have made almost every mistake you can make in accounting with my businesses. This tip will give you an overview as to what you need to know about the kind of business entity you may want to use with your business. Once you have a sense for your business entity, I highly suggest you talk to an accountant or an attorney who practices business law to ensure that you are using the correct entity and you do not overpay taxes. When selecting an entity for your business, first and foremost make sure you have protected your personal assets from potential lawsuits.

When it comes to lawsuits, everybody always thinks it's never going to happen to them. However, the truth is the United States is the most litigious country in the world. Meaning we are lawsuit crazy over here, and since it became legal for lawyers to advertise on billboards, television, and on the internet, the number of lawsuits has increased dramatically. It is not a matter of *if* you are going to be sued but rather *when* you are going to be sued if you are in business.

Different Business Entities

To begin with, we need to make sure when you start your business that you select the best entity that will provide you with the most protection from liability exposure and the best tax advantage. Some entities are sole proprietorships; some are limited liability companies (LLCs), and some are corporations. Each entity provides different tax advantages and different forms of liability protection. Be sure to discuss the protection offered for each entity and the corresponding tax differences with an experienced tax accountant. Creating the wrong entity can cost you and your business money that will go right to the government, because you were ill-informed.

―――――― " ――――――

Make sure your business operates as the best type of entity that will provide you with the most protection from liability exposure and the best tax advantage.

SOLE PROPRIETORSHIP

A sole proprietorship is easy to form and gives you complete control of your business. You're automatically considered to be a sole proprietor if you do business activities but don't register as any other kind of business.

Sole proprietorships do not produce a separate business entity. This means your business assets and liabilities are not separate from your personal assets and liabilities. You can be held personally liable for the debts and obligations of the business. Sole proprietors are still able to get a trade name. But it can be hard to raise money because you can't sell stock, and banks are hesitant to lend to sole proprietorships. However, sole proprietorships can be a good choice for low-risk businesses and owners who want to test their business idea before forming a more formal business.

LIMITED LIABILITY COMPANY

An LLC lets you take advantage of the benefits of both the corporation and partnership business structures. LLCs protect you from personal liability in most instances because your personal assets—like your vehicle, house, and savings accounts—won't be at risk if your LLC faces bankruptcy or lawsuits.

Profits and losses can get passed through to your personal income without facing corporate taxes under the business structure. However, members of an LLC are considered self-employed and must pay self-employment tax contributions toward Medicare and Social Security.

LLCs can have a limited life in many states. When a member joins or leaves an LLC, some states may require the LLC to be dissolved and re-formed with new membership—unless there's already an agreement in place within the LLC for buying, selling, and transferring ownership.

LLCs can be a good choice for medium- or higher-risk businesses, owners with significant personal assets they want protected, and owners who want to pay a lower tax rate than they would with a corporation.

CORPORATION

C Corp

A corporation, sometimes called a C corp, is a legal entity that's separate from its owners. Corporations can make a profit, be taxed, and be held legally liable. Corporations offer the strongest protection to their owners from personal liability, but the cost to form a corporation is higher than the other structures. Corporations also require more extensive record-keeping, operational processes, and reporting.

Unlike sole proprietors, partnerships, and LLCs, corporations pay income tax on their profits. In some cases, corporate profits are taxed twice—first, when the company makes a profit, and again when dividends are paid to shareholders on their personal tax returns.

Corporations have a completely independent life separate from their shareholders. If a shareholder leaves the company or sells his or her shares, the C corp can continue doing business relatively undisturbed. (When thinking of C corporations, think of Walmart, Apple, and IBM, which all have millions of stockholders.)

Corporations have an advantage when it comes to raising capital because they can raise funds through the sale of stock, which can also be a benefit in attracting employees. They can be a good choice for medium- or higher-risk businesses, those that need to raise money, and businesses that plan to "go public" or eventually be sold.

S Corp

An S corporation, sometimes called an S corp, is a special type of corporation that's designed to avoid the double taxation drawback of regular C corps. S corps allow profits, and some losses, to be passed through directly to owners' personal income without ever being subject to corporate tax rates.

Not all states tax S corps equally, but most recognize them the same way the federal government does and tax the shareholders accordingly. Some states tax S corps on profits above a specified limit, and other states don't recognize the S corp election at all, simply treating the business as a C corp.

S corps must file with the IRS to get S corp status, which is a different process from registering with their state. S corps also have an independent life, just like C corps. For example, if a shareholder leaves the company or sells his or her shares, the S corp can continue doing business relatively undisturbed.

TAKING ACTION

To get more detailed information about the different types of entities that best fit your business, contact an accountant or go to https://www.sba.gov/business-guide/launch-your-business/ choose-business-structure. This SBA site has some useful and easy-to-understand language on what type of entity may work the best for you.

Tip #7

SLEEP ON IT

What if there were a tool you could use to solve problems, come up with unexpected solutions, and drive creativity? What if I told you it would cost you nothing and requires very little effort to use? Interested yet?

Well, there is such a tool, and it's with you all the time. The subconscious mind is an incredibly powerful tool, but few take advantage of it. Your subconscious works throughout the day when you are both awake and asleep but takes over entirely when you sleep. Free from the interference of daily life and external stimuli, at night your subconscious mind has nearly all the resources of your brain at its disposal. With the subconscious mind dominating such a large portion of your life, you need to put it to work.

While sleeping, your subconscious mind will get to work, approaching any problems from a variety of angles and making connections that may hold the answers to these problems. When you are faced with a dilemma, know that you already have the solution within you. All that you need to do is draw it from your subconscious mind. Once you learn how to unlock the power of your subconscious, you'll have a powerful tool ready to go to work while you rest and recover.

Too many times we are too quick to embrace a concept or business opportunity without fully thinking through all the issues involved with the business.

I started doing this when I was told at a seminar to never make a financial decision that involves more than $1,000, if at all possible, on the spot. Instead, I was told to sleep on it and revisit the decision the next day because when we sleep on things, it gives our subconscious mind time to think through the issue and gives clarity on the issue at hand. Too many times we are quick to embrace a concept or business opportunity without fully thinking through all the issues involved with the business.

I have shared this concept with many people, and they have come back to me and told me when they first heard about the "sleep on it" concept, they thought it was silly and would not work. But once they tried it, they achieved the same results I have gotten over the years.

If you are anything like me, then you are an idea person. You have so many ideas coming at you on a daily basis that it is unbelievable, and you can't turn the ideas off. You will get ideas about everything. During the day, ideas about things you don't even care about will come to you, and you think you should act on them. Once I began to apply the "sleep on it" concept, it cleared through the fog, and I was able to focus and be more productive. Many times I will get these supposedly great ideas, write them down, sleep on the idea, and the next morning wake up and read the idea I had written down only to ask myself, "Was I on drugs yesterday?" because the idea was so nutty.

Knowing that it is easier to get into business than it is to get out of business, the "sleeping on it" concept is a godsend to help us keep our sanity and stay focused. So, why not allow your subconscious to go to work for you too? Once you try it you will be amazed how well it works.

TAKING ACTION

Before going to bed this evening, take a moment to think of a question you need answered or a problem you need solved. Then sleep on it and let your subconscious take care of the rest. You will be amazed how something as simple as waiting until the next day to answer a big question or make a decision will give you that much-needed perspective so you can proceed with confidence, knowing you are doing the right thing.

PART 2

Staying Competitive

Tip #8

PRICE AT OR ABOVE MARKET VALUE

Don't be afraid to price at or above the marketplace. Too many people think they can make money by selling for cheap. Unless you are Walmart or some other large business and have lots of staying power, somebody will always be able to sell cheaper than you. Slashing your prices is not a sustainable business plan.

If your business model is to try to sell cheaper than the other businesses in the marketplace with the same product or service, maybe you should be looking for a different product or service. The reason most other businesses aren't using this business model is because it is not sustainable.

Making money in business is about offering value, not providing low-value products and services. Always go for the high-value business and service, and you will separate yourself from the low-end providers.

———————————— " ————————————

Don't be afraid to price at or above the marketplace.

Find Your Niche

If you want to be rich, focus on a niche. A niche can be many different things. If you are in the food business, focus on one or two core products and become very good at them. Think of how McDonald's got started with hamburgers and fries and shakes. Dairy Queen would be another example with their signature products of ice cream. Federal Express has the niche of overnight delivery, and Domino's Pizza has the niche of delivering pizza in 30 minutes or less, or it's free.

Recently I came upon a business called Raising Cane's, which is a restaurant that specializes in selling only chicken fingers. This restaurant is producing some of the highest annual gross sales of any fast-food chain. Again, they are in a very small niche and doing exceptionally well. If you are in sales, you can focus on selling only one or two items, but you better be the best at these items.

I have sold hundreds (at last count just under 900) of businesses, but my specialty is selling convenience stores. There are people who sell only certain life insurance products or investment products. An added benefit to specializing in a niche is that you get very good at one thing instead of being a generalist, trying to be everything to everybody. When you specialize you become exceptionally good at one thing and ultimately become the go-to person in your chosen category.

Trying to compete with everyone on price is a losing proposition. As an entrepreneur, when you specialize in a certain niche, you can charge more than those who offer more general products and services.

TAKING ACTION

If you don't already have a specialty, take a closer look at your current business. What are your products and/or services? Then think about how you can offer them differently. Start making lists, jotting down words and phrases. Don't edit yourself. Just run with it. If you need some help, sleep on it, and let your subconscious work on it for you.

Tip #9

PRACTICE PRICE ELASTICITY

Whenever you can increase the margins on your products or services, do it. This is what is called *price elasticity*. Price elasticity allows you to keep increasing your price to test your market. When people stop buying, it's time to lower them a bit. In the world of products, customers will decide if your price is too high and will begin to shop elsewhere. If you are in the service business, money becomes an issue only in the absence of value. So, if you are in this industry, be sure you are providing the best possible value you can, and don't be afraid to raise your price, because if you are offering excellent service, you may not be charging enough.

―――――――――――――――― " ――――――――――――――――

Money becomes an issue
only in the absence of value.

―――――――――――――――――――――――――――――――――――

Besides, how do you really know what to charge? Of course, I am going to assume you have done your market research and checked to see what your competitors in your marketplace are charging because this is a given. If you have not done your homework, do it now. If you don't know your market, you have taken the first step to going out of business as you die a slow death.

Once you have researched the marketplace, then you can begin to inch up your prices until the customers either start to squawk or quit buying. A simple example is what fast-food restaurants do with the pricing of sodas. How many customers pay attention to what the price of a soda is when they are in the drive-through of a fast-food restaurant? Very few, I can assure you. Therefore, if your competitors are charging $1.50 for a small, $2.00 for a medium, and $2.50 for a large, what should you charge? The same? No, you would charge $1.65 for a small, $2.15 for a medium, and $2.75 for a large. Now, these are made-up prices, but my point is the customers are still going to be visiting your restaurant and are not going to go away for a few pennies. This same principle applies if you are selling services or manufacturing products. You never want to be the cheapest; you want to push the price envelope to the maximum.

I know for some people the idea of price elasticity scares them, but once they experience it, they find out they should have done it much sooner. When I was in the retail business and my cost of goods had increased, I knew I needed to raise my prices, but I was afraid to because I assumed my customers would stop buying from me. What happened was just the opposite. The customers continued to buy from me, and I was angry at myself for not raising the price sooner.

Sometimes the fear we experience in not being willing to increase the price of our goods or services is because we're stuck in the past. What goods and services cost 5, 10, 15 years ago is not what you should be charging now. Don't sell yourself short. If you haven't raised your prices in a while, do it. You'll be amazed at what the market will bear, and, like me, you might even kick yourself a little for not doing it sooner.

If you are fortunate enough to service multiple territories or marketplaces, then you can test a price increase in one area rather than rolling it out 100 percent to your customers. The point is to use price elasticity to obtain the highest gross profit you can so you don't leave money on the table.

TAKING ACTION

Research your market. What is the average price of goods and services in your industry? Then look at your prices. Are you competitive? Maybe too competitive? Give the numbers an honest look. If you haven't given yourself a raise in a while, it's probably time to do so. And if you are priced competitively and want to be making more, create a niche.

Tip #10

OFFER A FREE SAMPLE

FREE is a great sales incentive. One of the fastest ways to increase sales is to offer a sample of what you do for free. If you are in the food business, this is really easy by offering free samples of your products. How many times have you been in a Sam's or Costco store and run into someone offering you free samples of food?

Chances are it's fairly often. And you know why? Because it works. The same principle applies if you have a restaurant and have your customers try a new product or give away free samples of your signature sandwiches or dishes. Then there are the buy-one-get-one-free coupons that businesses distribute. What about a service business like an HVAC company? If that is what you run, you could offer a free duct cleaning inspection. Real estate agents offer free home valuations to prospective home sellers. You can also offer a money-back guarantee to instill confidence in your service with no risk to the customer.

"

One of the fastest ways to increase sales is to offer a sample of what you do for free.

One of my favorite examples of free is what we call the puppy dog sale. This is when a mom and dad with their children go into a local pet store to wander around and look at all the different animals the store has for sale, and they see a group of puppy dogs for sale. Of course, the children want to touch and hold the puppy dogs and find one they really like, but the parents are reluctant to purchase the dog. This is when the pet shop owner comes forward and tells the parents, as the child is holding the puppy dog, that he understands the parents' concerns about owning a dog and the maintenance and care that is involved with the dog.

However, the pet shop owner then presents the parents with a proposition. He tells the parents they can take the puppy home for the weekend and if they decide it isn't a good fit, they can bring the dog back at no cost and no harm to anyone. We all know the outcome of this story where the children fall in love with the puppy dog and show him to all their friends and make a special place for the dog in the house, and the dog becomes part of the family, and the pet shop owner makes the sale.

The same principle applies to the sale of automobiles by allowing the customer to take the car they are looking at home for the weekend, and the prospective buyer shows the vehicle to his friends and neighbors, and the customer ends up buying the vehicle. All because of the free test ride or free home visit. The list goes on and on, and it is because people love to hear the word free. It is one of the most popular words in the English vocabulary, so don't be afraid to use it.

TAKING ACTION

If you want to increase sales, try offering a free sample or trial to get things rolling again. Notice the response. Is this something you want to offer more frequently? If so, what steps can you take to work this into your promotional efforts?

Tip #11

THINK POSITIVE

Business is what you make it. Unless you have a terrible business with bad financials, then the business is you and your attitude. If you dread coming to work, your employees and especially your customers will recognize this attitude and will reward you accordingly. As Henry Ford said, "If you think you can or if you think you can't, you are right."

A lot of times business owners think they have a good business because the bills are being paid, the business is growing, and there is money in the bank account. To test this idea, reverse your thinking and pretend you are a prospective buyer for your business. What would you do if you were thinking about buying the business you presently are operating and own?

More than likely, you would want to know more about the business, and this is done by performing due diligence on the business. When a prospective buyer does due diligence on a business, they are sort of like a home inspector where they check everything out in the business. They will check the financial status of the business and make sure the books and records are accurate and in order. They will review any legal documents such as employment agreements, intellectual licenses, inventory of the assets used in the business, and the quality of the assets used in the daily operation of the business.

―――――――― " ――――――――

When a prospective buyer does due diligence on a business, they are sort of like a home inspector where they check everything out in the business.

Nobody said anything about selling the business, but it pays to act like a buyer and do your due diligence like you were a buyer interested in your own business. Because you may be surprised by what you may find out.

There is an old saying: "Pay me now or pay me later, but you will end up paying either way." You should heed these words now and cultivate a workplace that is positive so you don't end up paying later when it's time to sell your business. Some offices have what I call "stinkin' thinkin'," and the negativity in these places is palpable. If you don't nip that type of attitude in the bud, your business will be perceived negatively by prospective buyers, and you will make less (or even lose) money on the sale of your business.

The more positive you are about your business, the more people and employees will perceive the business in a positive manner. Positive thinking is contagious, and the upside of positive thinking is unlimited. Because it always starts at the top and in your business, you are the top person, and everyone who works with and for you will look to you for leadership and guidance.

———————————— " ————————————

Positive thinking is contagious.

As Thomas L. West states in *The Complete Guide to Business Brokerage*, the number-one reason business owners sell their business is because they are burned out.[1] The business can be profitable, but if the business owner is burned out,

---

1   Thomas West, *The Complete Guide to Business Brokerage* (Business Brokerage Press, 2007).

the only remedy is to withdraw from the business. If you are experiencing the "dread factor" where you are no longer enjoying your business, then be assured your employees, vendors, and customers will pick up on this and "reward" you accordingly.

TAKING ACTION

What three things can you do to create a positive attitude at work? Make a list and take action on these items as soon as you can.

Tip #12

KEEP YOUR COSTS DOWN AND YOUR OVERHEAD LOW

There is a difference between wants and needs. You may want new office furniture or a new vehicle, but you need furniture that is functional and transportation that is reliable. Knowing the difference between wants and needs can make you either wealthy or broke. When starting a business or operating a business, you should always keep Tip #2 top of mind: Focus on sales. Sales is the lifeblood of your business, and the costs needed to run the business are a necessary evil.

All too often a business starts to make some money, and immediately the business owner wants to buy new stuff because they have the money. All businesses are cyclical, meaning they go up and down. One day you are on top of the world making good money, and everything is going well. The next day? Not so much.

Life is cyclical. Don't fall into the trap of spending money you may need in the future on items that don't make you money. If something will not increase your sales or reduce your expenses and overhead, then hold off. The world is not going to come to a complete halt if you don't buy that new vehicle or furniture. Instead invest the money in something that will help you increase sales.

―――――――― " ――――――――

Don't fall into the trap of spending money you may need in the future on items that don't make you money.

One way to help you keep costs to a minimum and your overhead low is to live like a student. When you were a student, you probably wanted to buy many things but couldn't afford them, nor did you have room for them. Now that you're an adult with money to spend, don't waste it on things you don't really need. And don't do what most people do and build buildings for your stuff. Just because you have more room doesn't mean you need more stuff. So before you make another purchase for your business, ask yourself if the purchase is a need or a want, and budget accordingly.

TAKING ACTION

Do an informal audit of your business. Look at your expenses over the past year. Are you seeing any patterns? Are the purchases necessary? Or are there some areas where you can cut back? For example, are you renting more space than you need? If so, find a smaller space.

Tip #13

NEVER GO ALL IN

When you have a new product or service, never put all your money into one idea or product. Instead test the market or service before you decide to spend a lot of money on one certain promotion or a big ad. Test different markets with different kinds of media. Just because you like to get most of your information from Facebook or social media, other people may use a different kind of vehicle to get their information, so you will need to use an array of different vehicles to get your product or service to the market. The bottom line is to test, test, test. Because you are going to make mistakes. And it's better to make a lot of little mistakes than a few big ones, which could put you out of business.

---------------- " ----------------

Test the market or service before you decide to spend a lot of money.

Some of the top sales companies will come up with a new product or service or a sales area they want to test but don't want to spend a lot of money in the process. Companies used to develop a product or service, then put together a strong marketing plan and program and begin rolling it out to the general public. As products and services entered the market, businesses began tracking their marketing results. This is both time-consuming and expensive. But this was standard practice until somebody came up with the idea of test marketing the product or service in a limited area to see how well the public responds to the new product or service by using focus groups. If they get a strong response from the public, they discontinue the marketing and refine the product or develop the service based on the feedback they received before they launch the products and services. This ends up saving companies lots of time and money and results in better consumer products and services, which is a win for everyone.

Next time you have a fantastic idea that you think will sell, test it first with a prototype or sample service before you spend too much time and money on something that will not thrive in the marketplace.

TAKING ACTION

Are you in the practice of getting client feedback? This is one way you can improve your product and service offerings. If you aren't doing so, this is a great time to start. There are many ways to do this. One is word of mouth. Another is sending out customer service surveys to your customers. These surveys are designed to take the temperature of your business to help you see where you are doing well and where you need to improve.

PART 3

—

Understanding Partnerships

Tip #14

KEEP IT SIMPLE

Before you bring a partner into the business, first ask yourself why you think you need a partner. If you need a partner only for the money, be sure you have eliminated all your other possibilities with loans or investors first, because acquiring partners is like getting married to someone. If you need a partner for the financial side of things where they will put in money but won't have an active role in the business, then make sure each partner's role is decided in writing before you go forward.

> **Acquiring partners is like getting married to someone.**

I always believe in keeping things simple, and whenever you add more people to the equation, things become less simple and more complex. Without partners, you alone can make the decisions needed to grow the business or establish how the business is run. Add one partner, and now you must converse with your partner regardless of what percentage their ownership of the business is. Adding more partners makes the business and how the business is run only more complex. And please (I am warning you on this one) don't add relatives as partners. One of the quickest ways to ruin a relationship is to get into business with relatives. Money and relatives have a way of becoming polarized and the majority of the time do not end up on positive terms.

Regardless of whether your partners are relatives or not, generally what happens is one partner begins to think they are working harder or putting in more time and effort than the other partner and should therefore be receiving more compensation or benefits. And if the partners happen to be relatives, the damage caused from the fallout can be devastating and damaging to the family.

—————————— " ——————————

Businesses and relationships are easier to get into than they are to get out of.

What most people don't take into consideration is when they enter a partnership with someone in business, most of the time the partner will have a spouse, which increases the number of partners in the partnership. Even though a partner's spouse may not be active in the business, you can be assured they are active in their partner's life and will voice their opinion to their partner. I think you can grasp my point as to what can start out as two people entering into a partnership can easily turn into four people, which would be increased exponentially with the addition of another business partner.

Always remember businesses and relationships are easier to get into than they are to get out of.

TAKING ACTION

Are you thinking of adding a partner? If so, make a list of what you think the partner can bring to the table. Then make a list of pros and cons, taking into account what you learned in this chapter. After you have slept on it, as suggested in Tip #7, schedule an appointment with a trusted advisor, and discuss the pros and cons of partnership before you make any decisions. And if you are thinking of partnering with a family member, please sleep on it again. You'll thank me later.

Tip #15

USE A BUY-SELL AGREEMENT

If you are going to have partners, make sure you have a buy-sell agreement. Nothing ruins relationships faster than money and not having a buy-sell agreement. A buy-sell agreement can eliminate a lot of grief and costs if you have one in place.

These agreements are commonly used by sole proprietorships, partnerships, and closed corporations in an attempt to smooth transitions in ownership when a partner dies, retires, or decides to exit the business. The buy-sell agreement requires that the business shares be sold to the company or the remaining members of the business according to a predetermined formula.

For example, in the case of the death of a partner, the estate must agree to sell. To fund the purchase of the shares by the surviving partners, life insurance policies are taken out reciprocally by each partner on the lives of the others when the partnership is formed. These policies can be paid for by the company as a business expense, where the partners are the named beneficiaries.

"

Having a buy-sell agreement avoids costly battles for control.

Upon the death of a partner, the life insurance death benefit will be paid out to the remaining partners, who will use the funds to purchase the deceased's shares from their estate, ensuring continuity of the business and its ownership structure. Having a buy-sell agreement avoids costly battles for control with surviving spouses or children and having to use probate court.

Generally, when people get into a partnership, they are all getting along and having a lovefest. Then when the honeymoon is over—and especially when the business is not doing well—partnerships begin to crack and fall apart. Almost always the ruination of a partnership is when one partner doesn't think the other partner is doing their fair share of the work or responsibilities, and when the business is struggling these feelings are escalated. The same holds true when the business is doing well and is profitable, but the partners find this situation more bearable because each partner is receiving income, which lessens the bad feelings about a partner not carrying their weight.

———————— **"** ————————

Many relationships have been ruined because they didn't prepare a buy-sell agreement when the partnership was formed.

The worst kind of partnership you can have is when there is animosity and no communication between partners. In this scenario the partners are miserable but don't know why they are miserable because they don't talk about the situation between themselves. This is precisely when you will appreciate the fact you had a buy-sell agreement in place.

Many relationships have been ruined because they didn't prepare a buy-sell agreement when the partnership was formed. I have seen very profitable businesses fall apart because the partners got mad at each other and refused to speak to one another again but still owned the business together. It becomes a very cumbersome situation both mentally and financially. Don't let this happen to you. Always implement a buy-sell agreement in the beginning of the business partnership.

TAKING ACTION

If you are about to form a partnership, find a business attorney (if you haven't done so already) and schedule a consult. Explain that you need a buy-sell agreement for your business, and make sure everyone signs before forming your partnership.

Tip #16

BEWARE THE TAXMAN

Never forget you will always have at least one partner in your business, whether you want him or not. And that partner is Uncle Sam, who represents the United States Treasury Department, also known as the taxman. The taxman is everywhere. Local taxes, state taxes, federal taxes, sales taxes, withholding taxes, and several more depending on where you are located.

Paying taxes is one of the biggest line items that businesses neglect to factor into their business plan. Once you get behind on your taxes, it can be very difficult to dig out of the hole you have dug for yourself.

—————————— " ——————————

Paying taxes is one of the biggest line items that businesses neglect to factor into their business plan.

—————————————————————————

As we learned in Tip #5, a lot of businesses do not know that the taxman has rights that supersede your banks, creditors, vendors, and more. If you owe the taxman, it is not uncommon for the IRS to put a lien against your bank account and withdraw the money that is owed to them without telling you, whereby leaving your account short of funds, which creates a downward spiral of bouncing vendor checks and being late with employee wages.

This is why it is always important to factor in paying the taxman when you create your business plan. There is no way of escaping taxes that are owed to the taxman. And if you think filing bankruptcy will get you out of paying the taxman, think again. Generally, the taxman will be one step ahead of you. So, be sure to plan on paying your taxes, because the taxman is always first in line when it comes to getting paid. Failure to do so will put you out of business quickly.

I can personally vouch for having experienced the wrath of the taxman because there was a time when my controller had neglected to pay Uncle Sam in a timely manner, and without any notice from the taxman or my bank, the money that was owed to the taxman was withdrawn from our business account without our knowledge, thereby creating a deficient situation in the bank account, which translated into checks bouncing and vendors not being paid.

It is bad enough when something like this happens, but it is worse when something like this happens and you are not aware of it, because then you are working on damage control. If you are the one who is paying taxes, make sure you get them paid in a timely manner. And if someone else is responsible for paying the company taxes, follow up with them and make sure they get them paid.

TAKING ACTION

If you haven't already done so, create a payment schedule and set aside money for your business taxes, because it's the taxman's either way. Most people don't like the surprise of finding a negative balance in their accounts, courtesy of Uncle Sam. So plan ahead and save the surprises for birthdays and anniversaries.

Tip #17

CREATE VENDOR PARTNERS

If you are going to have partners, sometimes one of the best partners you can have is a vendor who is already providing services or products to your business. Think about it: You already have a good relationship with your vendor, otherwise they wouldn't be your vendor. The vendor also knows your business and how you do business and more than likely wants to do more business with you, so why not make the relationship a win-win situation for both of you?

By having a vendor as a partner, you can capitalize on the vendor's credit line and relationships they have within your industry. Your relationship with a vendor can be perceived as an extension of sales to the vendor. The vendor may need you as much as you need them, and since the vendor has a larger credit line with their lender than you do, this would allow them to give you and your business better terms on buying products, which is the same as getting a loan but not having to go to a bank.

"

Just asking a vendor to extend your payment terms from 30 days to 60 days is the same as getting a short-term loan.

More than once I have used my vendors to extend my credit line, thereby saving myself the hassle of having to get a line of credit from a bank to cover slow times in the business. I did this because my vendor was doing the same thing with their bank, and all I was doing was piggybacking off of my vendor's credit line.

Just asking a vendor to extend your payment terms from 30 days to 60 days is the same as getting a short-term loan. However, most businesses don't think about doing this. The truth of the matter is you and your vendor are already partners—you just haven't said it out loud or talked about it. Anytime you have vendors, they are nothing more than partnerships; the better you do, the better they do. They will always have your best interest at heart because they need you as badly as you need them.

———————— " ————————

Always stay close and in good graces with your vendors because they can help you when your bank won't.

Do you think Walmart or car dealers pay for all their inventory the day it arrives at their location? No, instead they use vendor financing. When companies get to be the size of Walmart or Costco, for example, they will dictate to their vendors what the terms are going to be. This will determine if they are going to pay in 30 days or 90 days. Depending on the size of your business, you may not get into the situation where you want to dictate terms to your vendors, but you do want to use their clout and financial capability to your benefit. Always stay close and in good graces with your vendors because they can help you when your bank won't.

TAKING ACTION

Make a note of your current vendors. Does one come to mind as a potential partner? Someone who you are on good terms with that knows your business and has your back? If you are serious about it, approach them to see if it is a good match, keeping in mind what you learned earlier about partnerships, buy-sell agreements, etc.

Tip #18

JOIN FORCES

There will always be other business owners who are in the same business you are in but not in your market area and not a competitor to you. So, why not co-opt other business owners who are in the same business you are in? This lets you capitalize on the knowledge of the group and possibly on the competitive buying opportunities co-opted individuals would offer.

"

Co-opt other business owners who are in the same business you are in.

People like to help other people—especially if they are in the same industry. Every industry has an association. Join the association for your industry, and by doing so you will get their newsletter and learn what other business owners like yourself are doing to make their businesses successful.

If you should read about another business that has some interesting ideas, contact them about co-opting on marketing or procuring products both businesses are using. If you don't want to join the association, you can search out other businesses like yours in a different trade area and contact them about co-opting.

To strengthen the idea of co-opting other businesses, I have many times contacted a business similar to mine in another trade area I had either read about or heard about and asked them if I could come and visit with them to see how they run their business. I was once in the Midwest and read about a business like mine in California that was offering some services to their customers I had thought about offering. However, I did not know how to implement the process and had never seen the process in action. So, I picked up the phone and called them and told them I was impressed with what I had read about their business and asked if I could come to California and visit with them.

They invited me with open arms, and I learned about their business. When I got home I was able to implement their ideas in my business, and it was a great success. The business in California knew I was not a competitor to them, and they were proud to share with me what they had created, so I co-opted their knowledge and experience, and it worked out great for both of us.

You will be surprised how many people are willing to help a fellow businessperson.

TAKING ACTION

Contact someone in your industry who is in a different market area. This way they are not a direct competitor of yours. Ask them for advice on ways they have increased their business and emulate what works for your business so you can profit from a proven method.

PART 4

——

Growing Your Business

Tip #19

BUILD YOUR BUSINESS SLOWLY

Most entrepreneurs love the thrill of the game and want to go fast. It sounds easy when you are reading about individuals who hit a home run with their product or service, and we want to emulate them. You don't know all the facts behind their success, and you are not them, so take your time to plan and execute your decisions. Building a business is like sailing a boat. A boat knows where it wants to go but is off course 90 percent of the time, and that is because it is constantly adjusting its sails to keep the boat on course. A business is no different.

―――――――――――― " ――――――――――

Most entrepreneurs never take the time to analyze what is working and what is not working.

―――――――――――――――――――――――

I was taught a very simple but effective way of how to build a successful business. First you analyze your business and find out what you are doing right and what part of your business is making you money. Next you find the areas of your business that are not profitable and may be costing you excessive money. Stop engaging in activities that are not making you money. Then go back and do more of what was making you money.

This sounds too simple, but most entrepreneurs never take the time to analyze what is working and what is not working and just keep blasting away and eventually lose focus. This simple example of doing what works and quit doing what doesn't work can make you wealthy and can grow your business exponentially.

TAKING ACTION

It's time to make one small adjustment to the way you are doing business. While my instruction is simple, do not be fooled. Practicing this will enable you to reap big rewards:

- Do what makes you money and stop doing what causes you to lose money.

- Audit your business quarterly or at a minimum annually, see where you are making money and where you are losing money, and do this exercise again.

Tip #20

BECOME A READAHOLIC

Read every book or publication you can about your industry or business. Very rarely are there any new ideas. Generally, people take a proven product or service and put a new spin on it, and based on their timing, it looks like a new product. Starbucks didn't invent coffee. They just put a different spin on it, and the marketplace embraced their concept.

Dominos didn't invent the pizza delivery business. They took a proven product and put a new spin on it with their 30-minutes-or-less delivery concept. Want to know how they did it? Read the books on the history of these and other companies, and you will get an idea as to how maybe you can do the same thing. Remember: Rarely are there any new ideas—usually they are only ideas that have been improved on.

An interesting and entertaining book you may want to read is by Joe Girard, who has been called the world's greatest salesman. In his book *How to Sell Anything to Anybody*, he tells the story of how he was so broke that he would have to park his car a block away from his house and come in through the back so his creditors who were waiting for him to come home would not see him and try to get money from him that he did not have.[2]

"

Rarely are there any new ideas— usually they are only ideas that have been improved on.

The straw that broke this camel's back was when he came home one night and his wife asked for milk for their baby, but he didn't have money to buy their child milk. The reason I share this story is to show how motivated Joe was to support his family and how creative he was when he started from nothing more than an opportunity to be a salesman,

---

2   Joe Girard, *How to Sell Anything to Anybody* (Touchstone, 1978).

not having any tools other than a phone book with which to build his business to worldwide success. Joe had previously been a builder but knew he needed money fast, and the only thing he could think of was to get a job selling. He came up with the idea to sell cars. He did not know anything about selling cars but thought he could probably learn how to. He went to multiple car dealers in his area, and nobody would hire him. Finally, in desperation, he convinced a car dealer to let him sit in the dealership without any pay and with only a phone book. The rest is history—he rose to win the number-one salesperson award in the country for the number of cars sold over multiple years.

One of the quickest ways to be successful is to study successful people. Seek out other stories that inspire you. For example, there are many YouTube channels and podcasts[3] with endless amounts of information about how to improve yourself and your business. I am not talking about the people who are trying to sell you some quick fix or money-making idea. Seek out content that is relevant to your success. One of the quickest ways to be successful is to study successful people.

---

3   Here are some to get you started: *Tony Robbins Podcast, How I Built This with Guy Raz, We Study Billionaires, The Tim Ferris Show,* or *Wealth Formula by Buck Joffrey.*

TAKING ACTION

Read *How to Sell Anything to Anybody* by Joe Girard. As you are reading, make note of any takeaways you can apply to your own business.

Tip #21

MAKE YOUR BUSINESS SCALABLE

Making your business scalable means you don't just have one avenue for making money. Think of the silver, gold, and platinum insurance plans, for example. This is one way to take the same service and add another benefit to extract more money for the core business. Another example is the car wash. When you pull up with your car they will have a sign asking you if you want the regular wash for $10.00 or the silver plan for $12.00, which offers something additional, and the offer continues up to the $15.00 platinum plan. This is one way to make a business scalable. The same principle applies to coffee or ice cream. You can take the core product and add additional toppings or flavors, increasing the sale price of the item and increasing your gross profit along the way too.

If you want to get more creative, you can take your car wash or coffee or ice cream business, and open additional locations or franchise the concept. This is another way to scale your business. What is not scalable is one person doing a job, and all they have to sell is their time. For example, if you are a lawyer or an accountant, unless you add other lawyers or accountants to work for you, the business is not scalable. Instead, you are an hourly worker.

There are many different ways to increase the sales of your business by using your core concept and growing off of it. Maybe a franchising concept would make your business more scalable, or adding representatives to sell or market your product or service in other areas of the country would do the trick.

———————— 66 ————————

There are many different ways to increase the sales of your business by using your core concept and growing off of it.

I mention franchising because all franchises are scalable. The franchisor has come up with a business model that is scalable and generates a profit. The franchisor then shares this business model with an individual who then becomes a franchisee, and they in turn take the same business model, implement it in another area, and pay the franchisor a percentage of the new business's profits. Some popular franchise examples include McDonald's, Jiffy Lube, Century 21, and Marriott, to name a few.

If you are not wanting to invent a new business and want to get a jumpstart on having a profitable business (and you have the net worth and liquidity to purchase a franchise), then franchising may be the right choice for you. I have been a franchisor and owned 10 national franchises. The key is to find the right franchise that fits the right area and follow the business model created by the franchisor. It is a plug-and-play model, and the percentage of success in new start-up businesses is much higher with a franchise than a new concept.

TAKING ACTION

Think of ways to scale your business. For example, can you add more product lines? Can you add more locations? Can you add more variations of value to your existing product? Pick the easiest one to implement first and do it.

Tip #22

KNOW YOUR MARKET

If you have a retail location, you need to know the demographics of the area you are servicing; otherwise, how will you know what to sell? Ask yourself, who are the people within one mile, three miles, or five miles of your business? The same applies if you are going to be selling a product online. You must know who your market is. Is your market young, old, rich, poor, rural, suburban, etc.?

"

You need to know the demographics of the market area you are servicing.

Case in point. When I was in the process of finding a location to build an Arby's restaurant, I was required to go to the national headquarters and corporate offices of Arby's, which at the time was in Atlanta, Georgia. It was a six-week course that every franchisee was required to attend to be awarded the franchise.

During the six weeks one of the required courses was a real estate course that talked about where you were going to build your Arby's restaurant, which had to do with site location. The Arby's corporation wants to make sure all their franchisees are successful because they receive a royalty payment from the Arby's franchisee based on their sales volume.

It was in the corporation's best interest to make sure you knew the demographics in the area you were going to be building your Arby's. They didn't want you to build an Arby's out in the middle of nowhere, but instead they wanted to make sure there were plenty of people near your restaurant and that they were the kind of people who liked to eat roast beef sandwiches. However, as we all know Arby's is not the number-one fast-food restaurant in the industry, even in today's world. This prompted the instructor of the real estate class to tell all the new franchisees—after doing all our research and market and demographic studies—to ultimately find a McDonald's and get as close as we can to them because they are the best at doing demographic research and determining who their customer is.

It is very rare you see a McDonald's restaurant fail, and a large part of this would be because of their research in the marketplace. The same holds true if you are providing a service to the public. You would not want to be offering a septic cleaning service in a metropolitan area, for example, because they have city sewer instead of septic tanks. Instead, you may want to offer a duct cleaning service in a high-density area of families who have clothes dryers.

It's important to know your market, regardless of the direction you take with your business. If you don't, you could end up trying to sell the wrong service to the wrong market. This will cause you to not just spin tires, but to spin them in the mud. By this I mean, you will be spending lots of time and money and not getting anywhere with your resources. As a result, you will very likely be out of business soon too.

TAKING ACTION

How well do you know your market? Do some research to see if you are well positioned or if you need to make some changes to your product or service.

Tip #23

KNOW YOUR CUSTOMER

After you have determined your market and buyer, don't forget about your customer. All too often a business owner will invest in marketing something they like that has nothing to do with the customer. It is like a business owner buying advertising on a rap radio station because they like rap music when their customers are country music fans. Sounds crazy, but it happens all the time. In other words, you want to fish where the fish are. Don't go fishing in the Gulf of Mexico if you are fishing for trout. You want to be fishing in the right place to begin with.

Sometimes it is good to role-play and pretend you are the customer of what you are selling and be critical. Ask yourself why anyone would want to buy your product or service. If you take a deep dive into what you are selling, you may find out you are the only one who is interested in your product or service. This is what we call making a deal with yourself, which also falls under the category of being delusional.

This is the reason large companies will do market tests throughout the country to confirm if their research was accurate. Think of someone being book smart vs. street smart. It's not enough to know *about* your market; you have to actually *know* your market (and the customers in it) before launching products and services if you want to position yourself for success. An example of this was when the marketing department for Coke, after doing an enormous amount of research, determined that the public was tired of the flavor of Coke and the product needed an upgrade, so they came out with what was called "The New Coke" with a new flavor. It is a case study on what not to do. The sales of Coke plummeted, and there was a public outcry to go back to the regular Coke, which is what they did. A most recent example of not knowing who your customer is would be the mistake that Anheuser-Busch made when they had a transgender influencer promote their Bud Light beer. By marketing to the wrong demographics, it caused the stock of Anheuser-Busch to drop 20 percent and impact the value of the company maybe forever.

TAKING ACTION

Do not assume you know who your customer is. Learn from the mistakes of Anheuser-Bush and others. Research and test and communicate with your customers. Find out what they really want and give them that.

Tip #24

RESEARCH YOUR COMPETITORS

No matter what type of business you are starting or running, you will have competitors. Even if there is no other business offering exactly what you plan to sell, there will be other products or services your target customers are using to satisfy their needs. Find out as much information as possible about what your competitors sell and how they sell it and what price point they are selling at. Competitive research is something you should plan on doing on an ongoing basis. Just because you did your competitive research on January 1 doesn't mean you are done for the year. Do it at least every quarter. Some businesses do it daily.

———————— " ————————

Competitive research is something you should plan on doing on an ongoing basis.

———————————————

Researching your competitors applies to all types of businesses: retail, manufacturing, online, and service businesses. If you do not know what your competition is doing, then you are operating blindly.

I have always been known to operate my businesses on paranoia. I am always looking over my shoulder to see what my competitors are doing and if there is something I can learn from them. I knew I wasn't the smartest guy in the room, and the last thing you want to have happen is to be blindsided by your competitor and then try to play catch-up. If that should happen it may be too late—your competitors have secured additional market shares, and you won't be able to catch up and may be on your way out. It is better to be proactive and constantly research your competitors than be complacent and get left behind.

TAKING ACTION

Create a competitive research schedule and start researching your competitors monthly or quarterly at a minimum. Each
time you research your competitors, write down one thing you
can do to set you apart from the pack and then take action on
that. It could be opening a new location in an underserved area
or offering competitive prices if you are pricing yourself out of
your market. Whatever you find is valuable. But what's priceless
is the action you take to make your business more competitive
and attractive to your consumer.

Tip #25

BECOME A
MARKETING MACHINE

There is an old saying that "timid salespeople have skinny kids." Basically, this means if you are not marketing to your customers, your profits are going to be lean as a result of fewer sales. While marketing and advertising can reach your target customer, you should never confuse the two. Advertising is when you pay a media company to distribute information about you or your business. Marketing is the act of telling everyone you know about what you do. This can be done through e-newsletters, social media, interviews (TV and radio), and inspirational talks about your business at your local Chamber of Commerce and Rotary Club.

Marketing can be fun and very effective. Never underestimate its power. Get creative. Tell the world what you do, what you are good at, and how you can create value for them. Don't be shy about letting people know you want to work for them and that you are good at what you do.

―――――――――― " ――――――――――

Tell the world what you do, what you are good at, and how you can create value for them.

―――――――――――――――――――――

Marketing is about connecting with people and staying connected with them and consistently staying in touch, which can be done in a multitude of ways. When you connect with customers on a regular basis, you will be top of mind when they need help.

TAKING ACTION

One of the best marketing gurus I have come across is Dan Kennedy. If you have not heard of him or his series of books *No B.S.*, then I suggest you go to www.DanKennedy.com or www .NOBSBooks.com. He is one of the most outstanding writers and providers of top-level marketing available for small businesses.

PART 5

The Importance of Networking

Tip #26

LEARN FROM THE BEST

Learning from others can help you improve your own business. Find mentors, join groups with like-minded people, and learn everything you can about your industry and what it takes to get from where you are to where you want to be. Attend industry conferences. Take training courses when they are available. Buy books and audio and video courses offered by experts.

"

Learn everything you can about your industry and what it takes to get from where you are to where you want to be.

Every industry has an association, including industries you have never heard of. For example, did you know there was a watch and clock association? All these industry associations consist of like-minded people like yourself who want to learn and share their knowledge with others. Joining an association is one of the quickest ways to get ahead in the business you are in.

One way to learn is to study successful individuals who are in the same industry as you—or who are in the industry you want to be in. One of the best ways I have learned to get ahead in a business I wanted to know more about was to find a successful business that was not a competitor and ask them how they got to be so successful. I wanted to find out their story and learn how they became successful. They were always happy to help, so give it a try.

For some people, buying a franchise is the answer. It is one of the quickest and most highly successful business models available to an individual who wants to be in business. I have owned over 10 different national franchises, and the reason I purchased the franchises was because I didn't want to reinvent the wheel. The franchise already figured out how to be successful with a certain business model, and if the business model worked in my target area, all I had to do was to apply the tried-and-true principles the franchise was offering for sale.

Plus, by owning a franchise, I was part of a group of individuals who were like minded and had the same goals and desires to make our business concept highly successful. With a franchise, I knew the franchisor would always be there to offer assistance and guidance with any problem I had because they had a vested interest in my success. There was always an annual convention where I could meet and talk with the most successful franchisees of the company. There also were regional meetings with other franchisees and ongoing communication from the franchisor on how to improve my business.

I am not promoting only franchises, even though I do believe they are one of the best business models to help ensure the success of a business. Whether it is through a franchise or an association you belong to, meet with others in your industry so you can keep on learning.

TAKING ACTION

Find others who are in the same industry as you but who are not direct competitors. You can do this at conferences or by setting up a time to meet or speak on the phone. This will accelerate your success and enable you to make fewer mistakes with your business by learning what did (and didn't) work for them when they were starting out.

Tip #27

NETWORK WITH YOUR PEERS

The saying "out of sight, out of mind" is true. People only remember what they have recently read or seen. Networking is a crucial component to your business. Join the local business clubs and associations that are available to you in your industry. If there is a Chamber of Commerce, a Rotary Club, or a Toastmasters club, join them. The same applies for some of the other national clubs and business organizations that may be available to you.

Networking with other businesspeople has multiple rewards. One reward is that other people will learn what kind of business you are in and may need your services. If you network with people at the associations and clubs and events, and people find out you are a plumber, a salesperson, or any other trade, there is a good chance they will contact you when they need someone like you for your services. But if you are not out networking, then the odds of getting business decreases.

———————— **"** ————————

Networking with other businesspeople has multiple rewards.

The other benefit that many people don't think about is what you can learn from other businesspeople who are your peers. Before owning your business, you may have been an employee, and if that was the case, you will have an employee mindset, not a business owner mindset, and there is a big difference. Your business peers have probably already dealt with employee issues, tax issues, vendor issues, marketing issues, and advertising issues. In other words, they have already made a lot of mistakes, and by associating with your business peers, you can probably learn more from them than you can teach them.

I know when I was an employee there were times when the management of the company I worked for would make decisions and implement policies that did not make sense to me. But once I became a business owner and associated myself with other business owners, the decisions and policies my previous employers had made and implemented made sense. What I learned from this was the business had not changed but my mindset toward business and employees had changed because now I was the company.

TAKING ACTION

Attend a networking event in your area. Talk to your peers and others who are in your industry. Pass out business cards and take cards from others. You may find a mentor out there or a new client. Make a point to network on a regular basis.

Tip #28

GET TO KNOW INVESTORS

If the business you are starting will need investors to grow, do what you can to find out where the investors are. Local angel investors and venture capital groups are a good place to start—attend meetings they hold or meetings at which investors are speaking.

Most communities have investor clubs or at least a Rotary Club made up of local businesspeople. Anyone in business loves to talk to other businesspeople, and if a good opportunity comes along, the money will become available.

———————— " ————————

If the business you are starting will need investors to grow, do what you can to find out where the investors are and where to find those who might invest in your kind of business.

You may be thinking you will never need an investor or investors. However, if you plan to grow and scale your business rapidly, then you are going to need money to fuel the growth. And where is that money going to come from? Is it going to come from your personal funds, from a lender, or from investors?

The funding has to come from somewhere. There are pros and cons to having investors. I have had investors, and sometimes they can be a real pain in the neck, and other times without the investors the project would never have gotten off the ground or become as successful, because I didn't have the money to keep the project going. I didn't get concerned about whether I would have made more money if I had owned the entire business myself, because I knew there would not have been a business without the investors.

I remember a friend of mine who was a real estate investor, and they were buying single-family homes one at a time when they could afford them or when they had enough equity in one property, which allowed them to borrow on the equity to buy another property.

They wanted to grow, and one day the opportunity arose when a fairly large apartment building came onto the market. They shared with me their desire to own the apartment building, but they knew they didn't have the financial capability to acquire the property. I suggested they find some investors and explained how to structure the purchase. Not only did they find some investors who wanted to own part of an apartment building, but they also were able to get the seller of the apartment building to carry a note for part of the down payment at a reasonable interest rate with interest-only payments, thereby reducing the monthly debt obligation and increasing the cash flow of the business. All of this was accomplished by adding investors to the mix.

Just remember that investors are partners, and partnerships are like a marriage with a lot of give and take. But they will work if all the parties involved are focused on the same outcome of making the business successful and profitable.

TAKING ACTION

Look at the growth of your business. Is it time to expand? Are you ready to scale? Get ready by researching local groups of angel investors and venture capital groups and making appointments to discuss funding opportunities that would benefit both of you.

Tip #29

KNOW YOUR UPSIDE

Before you engage in any new project or business, ask yourself, "What is my upside in doing this project or business? Am I just doing this because I see other people doing it or for my ego?" Be sure and run the numbers first. Do your financial pro forma, and if there is no upside, then don't do it.

All too often we get excited about a new business venture, and it appears to be a home run. It can be a new restaurant concept we have seen in another town or a new service business or retail business or online business. It doesn't really matter what it is, but you get excited, and you are sure it will make money. I know what that feels like, having owned over 40 different businesses. I used to see a business concept and pull the trigger without doing my "what is my upside" check.

------------------------------ " ------------------------------

If there is no upside, then don't do it.

Checking the upside means making sure it will not only make money but will also fit your lifestyle. For example, are there any unintended consequences you have not thought about? You may think the idea of quitting your job and becoming a salesperson to allow you more freedom with your time and family is ideal, but your spouse feels differently and says it won't bring in steady income. Then come the questions: What if it doesn't work out? What will we do then? Yes, the salesperson position has a beneficial upside in the short term, but is it a long-term solution? Make sure there is an upside before you make the switch.

The same would apply to starting a business. There are plenty of upside benefits in the short term, but does the business have the capability to grow and surpass your present income? If you are thinking of starting or purchasing a business, then research and find out what the average profit of the business you are interested in is. I have been guilty of going into businesses without researching what the average profit of the business was going to be, and the results were disastrous.

I once bought an Arby's franchise thinking it was a good

idea, built a new building, and started from scratch without doing my research on the average time it takes for an Arby's to become profitable. Had I done this, I would have discovered it would take five years just to start earning a profit and I would lose close to $250,000 in the process. The bad part about this fiasco is I did it more than once before I learned to do the research as to "what is the upside to this business" question.

―――――――――――― 66 ――――――――――――

If you are thinking of starting or purchasing a business, then research and find out what the average profit of the business you are interested in is.

Remember the first rule of business is not to lose money. And the second rule of business is to reread rule number one. Always check for the UPSIDE!

TAKING ACTION

Are you thinking of pursuing a new business venture? If so, do your research and make sure there is an upside before moving forward. This important step will not only keep you solvent, it will also help your business become profitable.

PART 6

Managing Employees

Tip #30

DON'T DO EVERYTHING YOURSELF

There is no perfect employee. If you are a business owner with employees, then you know it can be very frustrating trying to get employees to be conscientious and attentive to the task at hand and perform the job or task as you would. If you are new at managing employees, you may find yourself doing the job yourself instead of training the individual to do the job properly or replacing the employee. Since there is no such thing as the perfect employee, the best you can hope for is finding someone who will do the job 75 percent of the way you would do the job.

―――――― " ――――――

There is no such thing as the perfect employee.

I learned the concept of the 75 percent employee many years ago when I owned a chain of retail stores. I needed to beef up my marketing and went to the local print shop to order some marketing materials. The owner of the shop was a friend of mine, and as I was discussing the order with the person at the counter, the owner came out of his office and asked me what I was doing. I told him I had this new marketing concept and was ordering materials for it. He looked at me and said, "Don't you have a marketing person who works for you?" And I said, "Yes, I do, but I don't think they could do it as well as I could." That was when my friend said nobody will do it like you would and you don't want someone to do it like you would, because if so, they wouldn't be working for you!

Once I learned to adhere to the 75 percent rule when working with employees, it made my life as an employer much easier, and it will make your life easier too. That way you can spend the time and energy on training your employees to become the best 75 percent employee ever instead of searching for the perfect employee.

TAKING ACTION

Are you still doing everything yourself? If you have employees working for you, then let them work for you. Make a list of everything you can delegate to your employees, then train them, and use your "free" time to work on tasks more suited for a business owner, such as networking and business development.

Tip #31

WATCH FOR EMPLOYEE THEFT

This may sound like a crass statement to make about employees, but it is something you should be on the lookout for. The situation in today's world has become even worse and more obvious than it was 10 or 20 years ago with the availability of social media. We all know that an employee is hired to do the work they were hired to do. But employees have a tendency to let their minds wander, and depending on the job the employee was hired to do, the opportunity exists for the employee to not be fully engaged in the job and get distracted. This is the perfect opportunity for an employee to steal.

The Four Types of Employee Theft

Most of the time employees don't intend to steal, but they do. They tend to steal in one of four ways: time, product, money, or service. Employees may steal time by not working when they should be working. Or they may steal products from the employer because they feel they are not being compensated well enough and will get what they believe they are worth another way. Or maybe they will steal money if they are working in a business with large amounts of cash in hopes the owner will not notice. Or they may steal by providing the customers with poor customer service because they believe they are not being compensated fairly.

—————————— " ——————————

Employees may steal time by not working when they should be working.

The worst part is that you could possibly end up with an employee who steals in each of the four ways just mentioned. All of this may sound cynical, but after you have had employees for a while, you will realize this is a fact and part of human nature.

Once the concept of social media came into play, the genie was out of the bottle, and there is no putting the genie back into the bottle. Employees live and die on their phones. It is an addiction, and it is their life. Try to find one employee who doesn't have their phone in their pocket or on them at all times. If they are working in a retail or service situation, they are carrying their phone with them and checking and responding on their phone. If they are working in an office situation, they will have social media on their computer, or if that is not allowed, then their phone will be close by.

So, be prepared for the employee to do some type of stealing, and make sure you have the proper systems in place to deter any type of stealing or to minimize the stealing that may occur. As sad as it may sound, we used to build into our business model the percentage of stealing that we knew was going to happen, and it became a cost of doing business. It is a reality, so don't be shocked when it happens to you if it hasn't already happened to you.

TAKING ACTION

Take measures to address employee theft in your company. One of the easiest ways employees steal is by taking time from the company. These employees may be stealing your time by coming in late, taking long lunches, surfing the internet or social media sites, or leaving early. Address these behaviors early and keep an eye out for any future infractions.

Tip #32

GARNER RESPECT

The rule for working with employees is to always praise in public and reprimand an employee in private. There is no quicker way to make an employee lose respect for you or the business than by reprimanding them in public or in front of their peers or other people. Conversely, one of the best ways to improve employee performance is to praise them in public or in front of their peers. Remember employees need to be trained. And if you are not training them to act and perform as you would like, you have yourself to blame when results are subpar.

―――――――――――― " ――――――――――――

One of the best ways to improve employee performance is to praise them in public or in front of their peers.

One of the biggest mistakes employers make is not training employees on the employer's expectations. All too often the employer will reprimand an employee when they don't do something that should be a priority. This can happen if the employee is unaware of the employer's desires.

Since employees can't read your mind, I have something you can do to manage expectations a little better. Make a list of the 10 things you expect and want your employee to perform, in order of priority. Then ask the employee to do the same thing and have them create a list of the 10 things they think you expect from them in order of priority. Then compare the two lists with your employee.

What you will find is the two lists do not match each other. They may be similar in the tasks and duties that are to be performed, but the priorities of those tasks and duties may not match. When that is the case, it is nearly impossible for the employee to ever please you because you are not on the same page.

There is a simple solution to this. Share your priority list with your employee so you can both be on the same page. This not only increases productivity, but it also cultivates a more harmonious working relationship, paving the way for future tasks to be performed in the order expected.

TAKING ACTION

Whenever you have a new project, practice the list exercise that you learned in this chapter to manage expectations by keeping everyone on the same page.

Tip #33

HAVE A WITNESS

If you have to terminate an employee, never terminate them without a witness being present. Terminating an employee is an adversarial situation, and people have the tendency to have selective memories as to what was said by whom, and they will have a different interpretation of what transpired in your meeting with them.

Don't put yourself in a precarious situation because there could be accusations from a disgruntled employee. In addition to having a witness present at a termination meeting, always document everything that was said and have both parties—you and the ex-employee—sign off during the termination meeting.

TAKING ACTION

Hopefully, you are not in this situation right now. If you are, be sure to document what transpires and to bring that witness with you to the meeting. Be brief and to the point. And if they try to dispute the situation, cut the conversation short and ask them to sign the papers so you can both move on.

Tip #34

KEEP THEM MOTIVATED

Contrary to popular opinion, money is not the prime motivator for employees. Giving additional money to an employee will get the job done. However, complimenting employees and recognizing them for a job well done will motivate an individual much more than money will. Money works great in the short term if you are trying to hire someone or get them to do something up and beyond their job duties or even as a bonus to help keep them, but in the long term, employees want to feel wanted and appreciated and recognized among their peers.

———————— " ————————

Complimenting employees and recognizing them for a job well done will motivate an individual much more than money will.

A prime example of what I am referring to is the stereotypical government employee. Generally, government employees are paid fairly well and have a multitude of benefits, but they don't appear to enjoy what they do, nor do they seem to derive gratification from their work. The ones I have spoken with over the years generally hate their job, and all they talk about is retiring so they can go get another job with a business where they can enjoy what they are doing and feel appreciated and wanted. This is one of the reasons you see "employee of the month" photos or something equivalent to this recognizing their employees in a place of business. Employers do this because it works.

If you have ever been an employee, then you know what it feels like not to be appreciated. So, complimenting and recognizing your employee for a job well done and giving them visual recognition on social media or in the public eye is priceless and will win you a loyal employee for years to come.

TAKING ACTION

A little praise goes a long way. When an employee does well, let them know it. Show interest in them by taking time to get to know them. Do they have pets? If so, what about having a bulletin board with everyone's pets in the break room as a conversation piece?

Do they have any hobbies? Use this to cultivate team-building activities. Some examples include volunteer work. Let the employees vote on the organization they want to help each quarter and then give them half a day of paid time to support a cause of their choosing or the one that wins the most votes as a team-building exercise.

Do they like to cook? What about a chili cookoff or potluck? Do they like the outdoors? Perhaps a company picnic with team-building activities is in order.

Whatever you do, come up with a reward system that inspires them. When they reach their sales goals each quarter or hit some other benchmark that works for your business, reward them with an experience that acknowledges their interests and allows them to form a stronger connection to your team.

Tip #35

NEVER ASSUME

Assuming will always get you in trouble. Never assume anything, and I mean anything. Always give explicit instructions to your employees on how you want a certain job to be done. People who assume things are getting done or people are taking care of things soon learn this attitude will cost them and their business considerable amounts of time and money, unless they follow up to ensure that directions are being followed correctly.

"

**Assuming will always
get you in trouble.**

The assuming attitude can happen a lot to an entrepreneur who has worked themselves from the bottom of the business up to a management position. Since the individual knows what is supposed to be done and how to get things done, they naturally assume the people they hire know the same things they know and are just as conscientious as they are.

This type of thinking will get you in trouble every time. Instead of assuming, get the facts and the information.

TAKING ACTION

Reread Tip #32. And remember to follow up with your employees to make sure you are both on (and stay on) the same page.

Tip #36

BE ACCOUNTABLE

A little accountability goes a long way. Don't try to pass the responsibility on to someone else for something that went wrong and didn't work out. In business we always say, "Fess up when you mess up." The fastest way to lose respect among your employees and business associates and vendors is to not take responsibility for your actions. We all make mistakes, and without making them we would never learn.

Unfortunately, in today's world nobody wants to be accountable. Instead, they make up excuses as to why something did not get done or why it "wasn't their job." By not dealing with an issue that was caused because of your actions or inactions, all you are doing is kicking the blame can down the road until the truth comes out that you were responsible for the issue. And by then it may be too late because you have lost credibility.

"

Nothing builds trust and confidence in employees and associates more than someone who takes responsibility for their actions.

I remember one time I was dealing with a lawsuit and had to take the stand next to the judge while the opposing attorney asked me questions. I knew I was wrong but did not want to admit it—especially in a court of law. My attorney gave me some very good advice. He said not to try to dance around the subject or lie about it. Just admit and eat it (meaning fess up) and go on, which is what I did, and sitting next to the judge, I admitted I was wrong. However, if I had tried to lie about it and had not been accountable for what had happened, I would have dug the hole deeper and lost all credibility.

So, if you do something and it doesn't work out, admit it and move on. Nothing builds trust and confidence in employees and associates more than someone who takes responsibility for their actions.

TAKING ACTION

The next time you make a mistake (we all make them), just fess up. It makes you appear more human to your employees and sets a good example for them to do the same.

Tip #37

REMEMBER THAT YOU KNOW BEST

Don't listen to your employees when it comes to how to run your business. Of course, you want their opinion and need their feedback, but ultimately you are the owner and the one who is responsible for the well-being of the business and the employees. Remember they are employees, so don't let them make decisions about how they will spend your money. Businesses are not run by consensus. Employees can have opinions, and they should be able to share those opinions with you. But as the business owner you are not obligated to implement their ideas.

Getting out of business sometimes can be harder than

getting into business because of all the obligations you must make to get into business. As a business owner you are married to the business. You have an obligation to the business and to your employees whose livelihood depends on the business. You may have vendors whose business depends on you, as will their employees. But if you are an employee, you can walk away from the business anytime and not have to worry about the other people your quitting will affect. An employee may have a family or a spouse to answer to, but that is generally it, whereas the business owner has many obligations they are responsible for.

_____ " _____

As a business owner you are married to the business.

_____

In the operation of a business there can be only one alpha. One individual who is driving the train and is the visionary of the business. Think of Steve Jobs and his drive and vision for Apple. Think of Fred Smith, the creator and visionary for FedEx. Or Walt Disney, whose courage and vision created an entertainment empire. Yes, all these individuals had a lot of capable and talented people who helped bring them to the success they ultimately experienced, but they would have never achieved their success without the one individual who was the driver or alpha of the group.

There is always one person who has the ultimate say in any business decision. As the owner of the business, make sure that one person is you.

TAKING ACTION

Read about a successful CEO who inspires you. Learn from their leadership. Pick one thing you admire and incorporate that into your own business.

PART 7

Staying in Business

Tip #38

NEVER STOP LEARNING

What's profitable now won't necessarily be profitable next year or 10 years from now. So, don't let yourself fall into the "this is the way we have always done things" rut. Keep your eyes and ears open for new things. Are there newer or better ways to market your products and services? Are customers asking for something you are not offering? Is there a different type of customer you should be targeting? Get answers by reading everything you can about your industry and listening to your customers. Attend association meetings, conferences, and conventions. Know your industry and always be learning.

> "
> # Don't let yourself fall into the "this is the way we have always done things" rut.

One of the fastest ways to get ahead in business is to find who is the most profitable and successful person or company in your industry and connect with them. If you own a small business, such as a plumbing or retail business, then find out through trade magazines or associations who the top producers in your industry are and ask them if you can visit them at their place of business or take them to lunch.

This type of learning is very successful if the top-producing businesses you contact are in another part of the country and you are not a competitor. In these instances, the individual will happily agree to share with you how they have gotten to where they are today. People in general like to help other people—especially those who ask for help. This type of learning will increase your business and operations faster than any class or magazine you can read.

Something you hear a lot of people say is some iteration of the following: "I have been doing this for over 20 years, and I know what I am doing." Now, I'm not talking about people who have been in an industry for that long and have taken courses, attended conferences, and so forth to stay up to date on industry trends while looking for ways to keep learning and expanding their offerings. Of course, that is to be commended. We want experts in medicine, science, law, finance, education, and so forth. What I'm referring to are those who may be in the same industry, BUT they are still doing the same thing they learned two decades ago without updating their process. This is not mastery of a profession. This is stagnation. And stagnation is laziness and not to be commended.

TAKING ACTION

Research upcoming conferences or trade shows in your industry. Select one that you like and make a point of attending each year to stay current on industry trends. And if you aren't able to attend a conference this year, read a book from someone in your industry to gain a fresh perspective.

Tip #39

ALWAYS HAVE A PLAN "B"

You should always have a plan B, and a plan C if possible. I say this because things inevitably will go wrong, and when they do, you can't be standing there with your tongue hanging out wondering what you are going to do next. You always need a contingency plan so when something does happen the business doesn't implode and leave you with nothing to show for all your hard work. And worse yet, without an income.

―――――――――――――― **"** ――――――――――――――

You always need a contingency plan so when something does happen the business doesn't implode and leave you with nothing to show for all your hard work.

I believe you should run your business on paranoia. By that I mean you should be concerned every day about what can go wrong and how you are going to deal with it. Some scenarios look like this: People don't show up for work. Vendors are out of stock. Payables are out of control, and you are running low on money. People are quitting without notice. Your receivables are becoming slow payers. Your competition is starting to gain market share. Your bank gets bought by another bank, and the next bank won't make loans to your industry. The list goes on and on.

My point is you can't wait until something happens. You have to be ready for it and have an idea as to how you are going to deal with it. Chances are most of the things you get concerned about will never happen, but if they do you have to have a contingency plan.

Life is not linear. We do not live our lives in a straight line.

Things happen. People get sick. People get hurt in accidents. There are storms and tornados and hurricanes that can affect your business and your livelihood and your family, so you better have at least a plan B.

True story. On September 28, 2022, I was in Charleston, South Carolina, working on completing the sale of a large transaction involving a chain of convenience stores. As I was meeting with my client, the weather channel was reporting that Hurricane Ian was moving up the western coast of Florida and was headed for Sarasota, Florida. This was very concerning to me because I live on Fort Myers Beach, Florida, just south of Sarasota and knew the hurricane would be going past my house. After I left my meeting with my client, I headed to the airport to catch my flight back home but got diverted because—you guessed it—Hurricane Ian made a direct hit to Fort Myers Beach, Florida, becoming the second most expensive hurricane in history, literally destroying the city of Fort Myers Beach and surrounding towns.

The reason I share this with you is because I had a plan B in case this ever happened, so I was better prepared than others. Things happen in life we never could imagine, and there is no reason for their occurrence. They just happen. As the Boy Scouts motto says, "Be Prepared."

TAKING ACTION

What is your plan B? If you don't have one for your business, create one. And if you have a plan B, don't get too comfortable. Sometimes the best-laid plans fail, and you don't want to be scrambling when they do. So if you already have a plan B, revisit it. Is it still applicable? If not, make any necessary updates and create your plan C while you're at it.

Tip #40

BEWARE THE "DISMAL DS"

In addition to having a plan B to handle the unexpected in your business, it's important to watch out for what I call the "Dismal Ds." The Dismal Ds are significant life-impacting events that affect you and happen not just to you but also to other people in your orbit. You need a plan B for these too because the Dismal Ds are heavy hitters. They include whoppers like death, disease, dissolution of partnership, divorce, disruption of business from a competitor or the business changing, and sometimes from just doing dumb things. But the good news is that the Dismal Ds don't have to pull you down.

Sure, bad things happen. But how you react to them is crucial. Many times, the Dismal Ds will happen to someone who is not directly related to you or your business, but their effects will indirectly affect you and your business. Think of an employee whose spouse or family member has died or had a stroke or some other medical condition that requires them to relocate, reduce their time with the company, or quit altogether. The same would apply to someone who is affiliated with your business and gets a divorce or has a death in their family. An example could be one of your main vendors dies or is replaced by a new owner, and they change the terms of credit or how they do business with you. (I had this happen with a national company whose CFO made a deal with me on credit terms, and they terminated him and discontinued the terms of our agreement, which made my business unprofitable.) There are a lot of indirect situations that will happen, usually to an outside party who does not work directly for you, that affect you or your business.

If the Dismal Ds affect someone you depend on—like your bookkeeper or chief financial officer—you need to have a plan B to keep your business going. The larger your business is and the more moving parts you have, the more plan Bs you'll need.

TAKING ACTION

It's time to prepare for your own Dismal Ds. Make a list of 10 possible nightmare scenarios that could affect your business and the ways you plan to address them.

Tip #41

BE REALISTIC

There is no such thing as a perfect business. If you are looking at buying a business, you need to manage your expectations. Stop looking for "the perfect business," because it just doesn't exist. All businesses have what we call "some hair" on it. There will be some areas of the business you do not like. You have to remember that all businesses are fluid, meaning they are constantly changing, and sometimes the changes occur on a daily basis due to the market or the location the business operates in.

All too often prospective business buyers waste a lot of their time, their brokers' time, and the business sellers' time looking for the perfect business. If there were such a business, then it would not be for sale. And if you are selling a business, the same holds true in that you want there to be some upside for the new owner. Otherwise, it would not be in the buyer's interest.

———— " ————

No upside, no sale.

———————————

I once had a beautiful boutique hotel for sale in St. Croix, Virgin Islands. Everything about it was perfect. It had 90 percent occupancy. It was well kept and well managed and priced right. But I could not get it sold; every buyer that looked at it said the same thing. There was no upside because the business owner had done such a good job that the best the next owner could hope for was to maintain the present sales in hopes the sales didn't go down. In other words: no upside, no sale.

I recently had a chain of 10 convenience stores for sale. Six of them were good stores, three were okay, and one of them was a real dog. A lot of buyers were not interested in this package of stores because not all of the stores were to their standards. However, one buyer did see the potential in this package of 10 stores and bought them knowing he was going to get rid of the four bad stores by selling them to another operator.

The return on investment my buyer realized by purchasing an imperfect business was astronomical compared to if he had purchased 10 good stores. Why? Because if you are buying a business with good cash flow and that is all you are looking for, you will not experience an increase in the upside of the business, and without that your business will not appreciate in value.

TAKING ACTION

One of the most prolific authors on personal development that I know is Brian Tracy. Read or listen to his audiobook called *The New Psychology of Achievement: Breakthrough Strategies for Success and Happiness in the 21st Century*. It is simple, down-to-earth information that can be used today and make a difference while teaching you the upside of life and business.

Tip #42

BE PREPARED TO SELL

As a business owner you should always be prepared to sell your business. Often your business will be your largest financial asset, so it is not something you should part with lightly.

Knowing what your business is worth is no different than providing your banker with an annual financial statement. Just as your bank wants to know year to year how you are doing financially, every year you should have a valuation done on your business.

Too many times I have seen someone offer a business owner what seemed like a lot of money for their business, and the owner takes the money and leaves millions of dollars on the table because they never took the time to find out what their business was worth. Unfortunately, this happens more often than you would imagine.

"

Every year you should have a valuation done on your business.

It is also prudent to occasionally do what we call due diligence on your business. In other words, you should act like a buyer and ask the same questions of yourself that a prospective buyer would ask if they were in the process of buying your business.

For example, if you were buying a business, the first things you would want to look at are the financials of the business. Are they in order, and have they been prepared by an in-house bookkeeper? Or have they been prepared and reviewed by an outside accounting firm? You should also inquire about the following: Does the business have operational and human resource manuals for the employees? Is the business current on its payroll and sales taxes? Does the business have a staff of employees who can operate the business if the owner is gone or deceased? And lastly, is the business trending up or down? (The trend of the business will make a big difference in what buyers will pay for a business.)

TAKING ACTION

- Pretend you are a buyer interested in purchasing your company. What things do you notice? What can you do to make your company more appealing to a prospective buyer?

- If you haven't already done so this year, schedule a valuation of your business. You never know when you will want to sell and having that number in your head will help you get top-dollar for your business.

Tip #43

UNDERSTAND YOUR RELATIONSHIP WITH BANKERS AND LENDERS

Don't confuse bankers and lenders with friends. They are not your friends. Bankers and money lenders are in the business of renting money and nothing more. When they lend you money, they expect it to be paid back, and as long as you are paying back the money you borrowed from them, they will treat you like a friend, but the relationship is strictly transactional.

"

Bankers and money lenders are in the business of renting money and nothing more.

If you don't believe this, try missing a few payments to the bank or the money lender you borrowed the money from and see if they treat you like a friend. A friend would probably not have loaned you any money in the first place, because they are friends and want to remain a friend, but with a banker it is a business transaction and nothing more.

Also, if you don't have the money to pay back a loan, don't ask for one. And by all means don't go bragging to your banker about a great deal you found on a business or piece of property if you can't afford to purchase it. There is a good chance the bank will get the information from you and then tell you they can't loan you the money and turn your newfound opportunity over to the banker's friend who has the money and who will acquire your deal, thereby cutting you out of the deal altogether.

So heed my words: Keep the banker and the friend separate.

TAKING ACTION

One of the best books I can recommend that sheds light on business relationships is *Winning Through Intimidation* by Robert Ringer. Give it a read and go get 'em.

Tip #44

DON'T COUNT ON
FAIR-WEATHER FRIENDS

With regular people, we have friends, and we have acquaintances, or what I like to call fair-weather friends. True friends have your back. You can count on them. Acquaintances on the other hand won't drop everything to pick your kid up from school when you are running late. And I wouldn't count on them to pick you up at the airport.

Just like you shouldn't count on an acquaintance to help you when you're in a bind, you should never expect a banker to loan you money when you are down and out, and your business is hurting. Bankers are fair-weather friends. They want to loan money only to people they are sure are going to pay them back, and if you look like you are in financial trouble, they are not going to loan you any more money. While ironic, the rule of thumb is bankers like to loan money to people who don't need the money. And the people who have money know this and are able to get the banks to compete for their business.

—————— 66 ——————

Bankers like to loan money to people who don't need the money.

Even though the banker may know you are in trouble and are having some hard times with paying your bills and it is only temporary, they don't care if you are in financial trouble. They will still expect you to pay back the money you owe them. Trying to apply common sense as to why a bank would be pushing you to get their money back even though it may mean they don't get all their money back instead of working with you until you get things sorted doesn't make sense on the surface. But banks do not want to get in trouble with the bank regulators. This could cost the bank money in fines or force them to put money into reserves, which would reduce the amount of money they can loan to other customers. Or worse yet, the banker could get in trouble for loaning you the money in the first place, and they could possibly lose their job.

I recall one day walking into my local bank, and the bank president was sitting at his desk, and I asked him how things were going for him and if he had been making a lot of loans. To my astonishment he said, "You know, Terry, I could sit all year and not make one loan, and I would be okay, but if I make one really bad loan, I could lose my job."

Now isn't that quite an admission for a bank president to make? He was better off sitting in the bank acting like he was there to help his customers, when in reality he was concerned only about keeping his job. By the way he isn't the only banker who has confided with me over the years with the same fear. So, please don't forget they are lenders and fair-weather friends at best.

TAKING ACTION

Give Robert Kiyosaki's podcast, *The Rich Dad Radio Show*, a listen. His podcast covers a wide variety of financial situations including bankers and finance-related subjects.

Tip #45

ASK FOR MORE THAN YOU NEED

If you are going to be borrowing money, you have to know the rules. In the lending world, always ask for more than you need, because with lenders it is a game. If they know you need $100,000, they will loan you only $80,000. You are probably thinking that doesn't make any sense because you need the full $100,000. That is the problem. You told them you needed $100,000. However, if you had told them you needed $120,000, they would more than likely have loaned you $100,000.

Borrowing money is about collateral and equity and cash

flow. First, what are you offering to the lender for collateral? For example, if you want to borrow $100,000, what property or assets are you willing to offer the bank to assure them you can repay the loan? Is this collateral value more than $100,000? Or is it less than $100,000?

I'm asking you this because your collateral has to meet the LTV or loan-to-value formula the bank has established internally. Every bank has different LTV requirements. Some want a lot of collateral, and some will take a smaller amount. Sometimes if you have a good personal financial statement and are willing to give the bank a personal guaranty, the bank will loan you the money you need based on your personal financial situation. But for the bank to be willing to loan you the money, you must have a good cash flow income because the bank is really looking at how you are going to repay the loan. Even if you have a lot of collateral and a strong personal financial statement, if you do not have a lot of cash flow, chances are you are not going to get the loan, because lenders don't see how you are going to repay the loan without selling some of your assets.

If you think this sounds absurd, go ahead and try to get a loan for the amount you think you need, and see what reasons the banker comes back with to not loan you the money and what kind of reasons he comes up with as to why he is not going to loan you the money.

Remember that in order to get the money you want, you have to ask for more than you think you will need—even if it means paying some additional interest or fees. You should also have a plan for repaying the lender to assuage any concerns they may have about the loan amount.

—————————— 66 ——————————

In order to get the money you want, you have to ask for more than what you think you will need.

———————————————————

If you really want to get sophisticated about borrowing money from banks, you can do what I used to do. When I really needed to borrow money for a new business or another business venture, I would put my plan together as to how much I wanted to borrow and what I was going to use it for and how much if anything I was putting up for collateral and then I would go to the bank that I was pretty sure was *not* going to loan me the money. Why? Because I knew that when I got done with the bank, they would give me a list of all the reasons why they were not going to loan me the money and I could change my loan request, eliminating all the objections the first bank raised. Then I would go to another bank I was pretty sure would loan me the money, and the loan would go through because the first bank helped critique my loan proposal.

TAKING ACTION

The next time you are looking to get a loan, go to a bank with your proposal. If they reject your proposal, use their feedback to apply for a loan at another bank. This free critique can help you create a better proposal that will teach you how to play the lender's game.

Tip #46

STOP DIGGING!

When you are in a hole, the best thing you can do is stop digging. Not all businesses are going to be profitable. When that happens be realistic and review what has happened with the business, whether it has made money or not, and if it looks like it ever will. Don't get personal and let the business suck you in. Remember, you should never fall in love with a business or a piece of real estate, because it can't love you back.

66

When you are in a hole, the best thing you can do is stop digging.

If the business has continued to lose money for over a year, compare it to your business plan, and see if you did something wrong or if it is just the market. If the future doesn't look good for the business, then stop digging and close the business. Too many people continue to operate a losing business. It doesn't have to be anybody's fault; it can be just bad timing. Think of owning a restaurant when a pandemic occurs. There are no customers, and you don't know when they are coming back. You may be better off closing the business, accepting the losses, and moving on. There will be more opportunities later.

All too often business owners who have been losing money over a long period of time have a tendency to cling to false hope and think if they do such and such or add certain things to the business, things will turn around and their business will be profitable. I'm here to tell you that just won't happen. The numbers don't lie, so why keep deluding yourself?

I remember consulting with the owner of a convenience store, and after reviewing his financial statements, I noticed he had been losing money for over three years. My advice? I told the owner he needed to close the store and cut his losses. His response to me was he was going to begin selling pizza and that would make the store profitable. Having been in the pizza business, I asked him how many pizzas he planned to sell a week. When he gave me a number, I did the math for him based on the number of sales he anticipated. I showed him what the gross profit for the year would be and how even with adding the sales of pizza the store would still be losing money. It was only after my demonstration of the pizza pro forma that he came to his senses and decided to close the store.

After a business has lost money for over a year, it may take two to three years just to get back to the break-even point. This makes it even harder for a business to become profitable. And most businesses don't have the luxury of time. I understand how hard it is to close a business, having been there more than once. But one thing I can tell you for sure is the first time you make the decision to close a business, it is excruciatingly hard, but after the first time it becomes easier, and there has never been a time when I closed a business that I regretted it. My only regret was that I didn't close the business sooner, and I know you will feel the same way after you have to close a business.

TAKING ACTION

Take an honest assessment of your business. Are you turning a profit or losing money? Then ask yourself how long this has been going on. If you have been losing money consistently over the past year (or more), it's time to stop digging and shutter your establishment.

Tip #47

KEEP YOUR BUSINESS TO YOURSELF

Keep your business to yourself and with only the people who are involved. Anything other than talking with your accountant or partners about the profitability of the business can be considered either bragging or whining or complaining. Nobody who is not directly involved with your business wants to hear about your business. Unless you are working with a mentor who is either more experienced or wealthier than you, why would you talk to someone about your business? Because if they are not on the same level of business you are and have the same desires to increase the size and profitability of your business, why would you be talking to them?

If you are going to talk to anyone about your business, make sure it is with someone who can add value and help bring you up in a positive way by encouraging you to continue to learn and grow your business, not someone who is less accomplished than you. In life we want to surround ourselves with people who can help us to improve ourselves, our situation, and our business, not a bunch of naysayers or someone who is unversed in the art of business.

"

If you are going to talk to anyone about your business, make sure it is with someone who can add value.

I have worked with many successful businesspeople who were making millions of dollars a year from their business, and even though they all had lots of friends with whom they played golf or tennis, they were not able to talk with them about business, because they were not versed in the area of business. Their friends may have been doctors and lawyers and the like, but they were not business owners and could not relate to the same experiences and issues a business owner must address on a daily basis. These business owners would welcome the time we would spend together going to lunch and dinner because they had me to talk to about their business. I understood what they were experiencing, and I was encouraging them to continue to improve their business and was commending them on what they had accomplished. I knew how much they were making in a year, and I was glad for them.

However, someone who is not familiar with how hard it is to own and operate your own business would probably see the amount of money these individuals were making and become jealous or worse, let it affect their relationship as friends. All the more reason not to mix business and friends.

TAKING ACTION

Make a list of colleagues (and mentors) you can talk shop with. Make it a practice to share only with those who understand your work and want to see you succeed.

Tip #48

TAKE INVENTORY OFTEN

When someone hears the word inventory, they generally think of a retail business, and most of the time they would be correct. Regardless of whether the business is retail or not, you need to take an inventory of your business on a regular basis.

If you are in retail, you must take inventory each month (at a minimum), not annually like some businesses I know. Not taking inventory is another way to lose money, and it is nobody's fault but your own for not staying on top of your business. Inventory affects cash flow, and cash flow is the lifeblood of any business.

Taking inventory of the business also includes the employees of the business. Do you need all the people you have on the payroll? Are you carrying too much in receivables? Are you paying too much for utilities or insurance? All these items consist of taking inventory of your business.

———————— " ————————

Inventory affects cash flow, and cash flow is the lifeblood of any business.

It is too easy to be content with the way things are running. One day things change, and you are not as profitable as you were in the past, and you don't know why. However, if you are always taking inventory of your employees, your assets, your bookkeeping, your payroll—basically everything related to the business—then you will know where you stand on a daily basis.

TAKING ACTION

Add inventory as an action item to your calendar. Get into the habit of taking inventory each month to ensure that you are running lean and retaining as much profit as you can.

Tip #49

KEEP SETTING GOALS

Goals are a road map for your business. In your business you will want to set financial goals, management goals, and leadership goals with deadlines. All of these goals must be in writing and have a target date so you can monitor your progress. You should create a combination of short-term goals (to complete each day, week, and month), mid-term goals (to complete each quarter), and long-term goals (to complete each year).

It is gratifying to see how far you have come. But you won't see the journey if you don't track it. A business without goals cannot expect to accomplish its full potential.

Setting financial goals should be the easiest of all goals to set. Sales goals are always at the top of the list, but don't forget to set profit goals. People goals are constant. You should evaluate your employees regularly. How are they performing? Are they still in the learning process? Are they cross-trained so you can be prepared in case you should experience the Dismal Ds?

———————————— 66 ————————————

A business without goals cannot expect to accomplish its full potential.

Remember, goals are your business scorecard. It is important to keep score regularly so you can monitor all aspects of running your business. Are you getting straight As? Great. Any Bs or Cs? Time to evaluate. Any Ds or Fs? Time to take action.

TAKING ACTION

Create a business scorecard. List your goals and add a due date next to them. Visit the scorecard each month to see how you are doing and if there are any new goals you can set.

Tip #50

KNOW YOUR BUSINESS

It's important to know what kind of business you are really in. For example, McDonald's appears to be in the business of selling hamburgers and sandwiches, and that is true if you are a McDonald's franchisee. But the company McDonald's is actually in the real estate business. The McDonald's business model is set up so that McDonald's owns the property, which they rent to their franchisee. The rent the franchisee pays is a percentage of the restaurant. Plus, McDonald's also get a royalty percentage of any sales of their products within the store.

While McDonald's is in the real estate business, Dairy Queen is in the proprietary product business. When Dairy Queen sells an individual a franchise, DQ gets paid a franchise fee. In this business model the franchisee owns (or leases) the real estate, but the franchisee pays DQ a percentage of their sales as a royalty. The franchisee must also buy the proprietary ice cream mix from Dairy Queen, which is another profit center for DQ. And the franchisee can purchase their restaurant equipment only from approved DQ vendors where DQ makes a profit from the sale of the equipment.

Another example is Amazon, the giant online retailer. They sell stuff, right? Did you know that over 50 percent of Amazon's income is derived from Amazon Web Services, a subsidiary of Amazon that provides online web services to third-party vendors?[4]

Look at Visiting Angels. They appear to be in the business of caregiving for elderly people. While they do that indirectly, they are actually in the temporary personnel business for individuals who need personal care.

And when I am engaged with a client selling their business, it appears on the surface that I am a broker or intermediary in the sale of their business, which is partially true. But the real business I am in is the ability to solve the problems my clients have when it comes time to sell their business.

---

4   Aran Ali, "AWS: Powering the Internet and Amazon's Profits," *Visual Capitalist*, July 10, 2022, https://www.visualcapitalist.com/aws-powering-the-internet-and-amazons-profits/.

I'm sharing this with you because the kind of business you are in can get lost in the day-to-day minutia of details and disruptions that come with operating a business. We are all in the business of solving problems for different situations. And the bigger the problems we solve, the more value we create and the more compensation that is involved.

For example, imagine you are an attorney who specializes in intellectual property for the movie industry. Chances are the problems you are working on will be of very high value, and the compensation you receive will reflect this service. The same principle applies to someone who is a plumber. When the toilets and showers in your house won't drain, you have a problem, and the amount of money you will pay to fix this problem increases every minute you wait to find a plumber.

"

The bigger the problems we solve, the more value we create and the more compensation that is involved.

So, stand back and really look at what kind of business you are in. This will help you to understand how you can improve your situation. Bigger problems equal more opportunity. What big problems are you going to solve today?

TAKING ACTION

Do you know what kind of business you are really in? Look at what you offer on the surface, then drill down. At the center you will find your real answer. Once you know that, look at the level of problems you are solving. Is there an opportunity to solve even bigger problems?

Bonus Tip

NEVER FORGET WHY YOU GOT INTO BUSINESS

Not everybody is wired to be in business for themselves. Most people are better suited to having a job, which is okay, and there is nothing wrong with that. But the people who decide to go into business for themselves have an ulterior motive.

"

Not everybody is wired to be in business for themselves.

And that ulterior motive is generally to give themselves more options in their life so they can have more freedom and control over their time and income. Most business owners work 24 hours a day. If they are not at their place of business, then they are thinking about their business because they enjoy what they are doing and accomplishing.

Never forget why you are in business for yourself; it will keep you motivated and going when times get rough. Remember you can always get a job, but getting into business is a journey. Being a business owner sets you apart from the crowd, and you should stand proud as a business owner, regardless of whether the business was a success or not.

I have owned over 40 different businesses, and the majority of them were not profitable businesses. However, I wouldn't trade the experience of owning those businesses for anything, because the businesses I owned that were successful would not have been successful without the ones that weren't. So, enjoy the journey of being a business owner, and profit from the lessons you learn along the way.

TAKING ACTION

Find an object that serves as a constant reminder of why you started your own business and place it somewhere prominent at work. It could be a poster of your mission statement, an award you won, or a picture of your family. Whatever it is, place it some-where you will see it every day. It should be something that makes you proud. At the beginning and end of your workday, pat yourself on the back. You did it. Now keep it up!

CONCLUSION

Throughout this book I have shared the top 50 tips to becoming a successful entrepreneur. I wrote this book to give you an overall picture of things you will need to keep in mind if you are going to be in business.

However, the one item I did not mention that will guarantee to make you a success in business is the desire and attitude you have toward wanting to be in business. I mentioned in the Preface that I had a desire to be in business for myself from the time I was in grade school. I always knew I was going to be in business someday, and I never lost that desire.

My attitude toward business changed as I matured and realized what worked and didn't work, but my desire has never waned. Instead, it continues to grow stronger each day, which is why I like to share all the knowledge and experience I have garnered.

The decision to be in business for yourself can be twofold. Maybe you want to be in business because of the lifestyle you desire. That is a wonderful way to live your life because the goal is to make your vocation your vacation so you never have to go to work. Or your desire to be in business may be to make as much money as you can because you want to improve things for yourself and your family, which is a good thing too. Or if you are like me, you want to be your own boss and make as much money as you can, and you treat business as a game and have fun along the way.

Regardless of your motivation for wanting to be in business, it will always come back to your desire, because without the desire to do anything, you will never be successful at the level you aspire to.

So, now that you have this knowledge, it is time to apply it to your own business so you can profit from my experience and hopefully avoid some of the hard lessons I learned over the years. Either way it will be a great journey and you will learn a lot about yourself, how to treat other people, and how people will treat you once you become a business owner instead of an employee. Being in business is not for the faint of heart; however, if you stick with it, you will come out a stronger, more defined, and more confident individual.

ABOUT THE AUTHOR

Terry Monroe is the founder and president of American Business Brokers & Advisors (ABBA) and is a four-time author. His most recent book is titled *Hidden Wealth: The Secret to Getting Top Dollar for Your Business* with Forbes Books. Monroe has owned and operated more than 40 different businesses, sold over 900 businesses, and worked with more than 1,000 buyers and business owners. As president of American Business Brokers & Advisors, which he founded in 1999, he serves as an advisor to business buyers and sellers throughout the nation. As an expert source, he has been written about and featured in the *Wall Street Journal*, *Entrepreneur* magazine, *CNN Money*, *USA Today*, *CEOWORLD*, and *Forbes*. Terry enjoys sharing his experiences both as a professional intermediary and as a business owner. The tips he shares in this book are based on his own "expensive experiences." It is Terry's hope that others will profit from his mistakes so they can avoid the costly dues of time, grief, and money that he paid along the way. To learn more about Terry, visit www.TerryMonroe.com.

www.ingramcontent.com/pod-product-compliance
Lightning Source LLC
Chambersburg PA
CBHW030504210326
41597CB00013B/788